PRAISE FOR *THE NURTURE METHOD*

"For over a decade parents have asked me how to practice mindfulness when you have a baby, and Lindsay Ambrose and Arden Joy have answered that question far better and more thoroughly than I ever could have. *The Nurture Method* is exactly what new parents need to bring them through the infant turmoil feeling grounded and providing their child with the very best thing they can: their *presence*. *The Nurture Method* is a practical guide to cutting through the chaos and distraction with mindfulness without adding a single to-do to a parent's full plate. I highly recommend it!"

—**Hunter Clarke-Fields, author of *Raising Good Humans* and host of the Mindful Parenting Podcast**

"If you're looking for a more peaceful and connected approach to parenting your baby, then this is the book for you! Amid the whirlwind of raising a little one, it's easy to slip into autopilot. *The Nurture Method* offers thoughtful insights and gentle guidance on blending mindfulness with parenting to nurture happy, secure, and resilient infants. A must-read for any new parent!"

—**Bex Band, author of *Three Stripes South*, *Family Adventures*, and *Gather* and founder of Love Her Wild**

"This book feels like a breath of relief to an overwhelmed new parent's nervous system. The magic of *The Nurture Method* is that it is as much about parents nurturing ourselves as it is about practicing mindfulness with our children. New parents, this book will be the gem of your middle-of-the-night reading pile."

—**Jessie Everts, PhD, LMFT, author of *Brave New Mom***

"As a new parent, one of the hardest things I remember was trying to find the vocabulary needed to explain the challenges I was having. Lindsay and Arden do an exceptional job of helping a new generation of parents not only find those words but also find some stillness in the beautiful chaos of early childhood development. I wish I had access to this book ten years ago when we were looking for mindfulness."

—**Elizabeth Nelson, influencer, Geek Girl Travel**

"*The Nurture Method* by Lindsay Ambrose and Arden Joy is a must for all expecting and experienced families. There are so many gems within the book that I will be sharing with expectant families and be integrating into my own family. The book's perspective is a perfect combination of holistic and practical."

—**Anna Rodney, owner and founder of Chicago Family Doulas and Birth and Baby University**

"Families across the United States are desperate for the kind of practical, easy, and accessible methods presented in *The Nurture Method*. They've always sought mindfulness but after everything people have been through with the pandemic, the desire is greater than ever. The world needs *The Nurture Method* right now!"

—**Laura Stotland, influencer and founder of Local Anchor**

"Successful parenting requires wisdom and the right methods. This unique book offers an amazing toolkit to tackle the complex challenge of parenting. It is called the Nurture Method, a treasure chest that encompasses simple and effective tools that parents can begin applying from day one, as well as the practice of mindfulness that is deemed the best thing that a parent can do for their children."

—**Mei-Wei Chen, PhD, psychologist and professor of counseling at Northeastern College**

"As a physician and mother, I value this evidence-based approach to raising children in a connected and calm environment. I recommend mindfulness when discussing anxiety with my patients and *The Nurture Method* offers a much-needed guide to help during the stressful first years of parenthood."

—**Lisa Ravindra, MD, FACP, assistant professor of internal medicine, Rush University Medical Center**

"Yes, this book is good for babies, but it is an even better reminder that we can all benefit when we turn off our autopilot and parent in the present."

—**Jacob Grant, author and illustrator of *Umami***

"*The Nurture Method* is user-friendly and offers practical mindfulness tips for everyday life, especially for parents. The authors suggest treating the book like a 'buffet' to customize your mindfulness practice and view intention as a flexible path. As a mom who faced postpartum anxiety, I wish I'd had this guide then, and I'm glad to have it now for my ongoing parenting journey."

—**Michelle Howell, Certified Educator of Infant Massage**

The Nurture Method

Mindful Parenting with Babies

Lindsay Ambrose
Arden Joy

BLOOMSBURY ACADEMIC
NEW YORK • LONDON • OXFORD • NEW DELHI • SYDNEY

BLOOMSBURY ACADEMIC
Bloomsbury Publishing Inc, 1385 Broadway, New York, NY 10018, USA
Bloomsbury Publishing Plc, 50 Bedford Square, London, WC1B 3DP, UK
Bloomsbury Publishing Ireland, 29 Earlsfort Terrace, Dublin 2, D02 AY28, Ireland

BLOOMSBURY, BLOOMSBURY ACADEMIC and the Diana logo are
trademarks of Bloomsbury Publishing Plc

First published in the United States of America 2025

Copyright © Bloomsbury Publishing, 2025

Cover image: © istock/Liubov Mahda

All rights reserved. No part of this publication may be: i) reproduced or transmitted in any form, electronic or mechanical, including photocopying, recording or by means of any information storage or retrieval system without prior permission in writing from the publishers; or ii) used or reproduced in any way for the training, development or operation of artificial intelligence (AI) technologies, including generative AI technologies. The rights holders expressly reserve this publication from the text and data mining exception as per Article 4(3) of the Digital Single Market Directive (EU) 2019/790.

Bloomsbury Publishing Inc does not have any control over, or responsibility for, any third-party websites referred to or in this book. All internet addresses given in this book were correct at the time of going to press. The author and publisher regret any inconvenience caused if addresses have changed or sites have ceased to exist, but can accept no responsibility for any such changes.

A catalog record for this book is available from the Library of Congress.

ISBN: HB: 979-8-88180-719-1
ePDF: 979-8-76516-523-2
eBook: 979-8-88180-720-7

Typeset by Deanta Global Publishing Services, Chennai, India
Printed and bound in the United States of America

For product safety related questions contact productsafety@bloomsbury.com.

To find out more about our authors and books visit www.bloomsbury.com
and sign up for our newsletters.

Definition: nur·ture meth·od (/ˈnərCHər/ /ˈmeTHəd/)

Noun
A practical methodology and set of techniques for being more mindful and present with babies.

Verb

1. To sprinkle mindfulness into the chaos of the day with babies.
2. To connect with your little one in a special way and give them a foundation of mindful practices that will support them for the rest of their life.

Contents

Prologue	ix
How to Use This Book	xi

Part 1: Mindfulness and the Nurture Method — 1

1. Exploring Mindfulness — 3
2. The Nurture Method — 19

Part 2: Techniques — 37

3. Words — 39
4. Songs — 51
5. Mantra — 61
6. Breath — 69
7. Space — 81
8. Play — 89
9. Adventure — 101
10. Ritual — 113
11. Sleep — 127
12. Energy — 143

Part 3: Integrating the Nurture Method — **163**

13 Okay, Now What — 165

14 Nurture in Action: NEST — 173

15 What to Do When . . . — 187

Epilogue — 191

Notes — 193

Index — 199

About the Authors — 201

Prologue

THE CORE INGREDIENT

There is a core component at the heart of the Nurture Method. It's the core because in the eyes of your baby, it's all there is.
Ready for it?
It's you.
Your presence, attention, and love are what your baby needs most. In a world where *what you have* and *what you do* have taken the focus, it's easy to forget that *simply being* with your baby is the greatest gift you can give. Your baby doesn't care if you know what you are doing, what you look like, what you have or don't have, what you have accomplished or not. Your baby just wants you, *as you are*.

But taking care of a baby is hard and being there, as you are, is no easy task. In fact, research shows that happiness in parenthood often goes down significantly in the early years of having a child (more than loss of a loved one to death or divorce—yeah, parenting is *that* hard). That statistic probably comes as no surprise. Because not only are you elbows deep in diapers and sleep deprivation, you're having to manage all that while trying to figure out *what the heck is going on* which is constantly changing because your baby is someone new practically every day. And for some reason there's a ubiquitous misconception that figuring out what the heck is going on and knowing how to navigate it as a Nurturing parent comes naturally. But that's just not the case. Yes, of course, we love our little ones but parenting is a skill and, like anything else, parents need to *learn the skills to be present and create these essential early, positive interactions with their baby.*

At the same time that you're trying to figure everything out, your baby is looking to you for cues on how to respond, interact, and show up in the world. Over 80 percent of their brain structure develops between ages zero and five,[1] meaning your little one is learning from day one, soaking up everything like a sponge. Your little ones need you to be present, attentive, and loving and how you show up will create neural connections that contribute to their brain development and shape their understanding of love and relationships.

So, what can we do?

We *know* that mindfulness can help. Many studies over many years have shown that mindfulness in parenting can help us cultivate the presence and awareness needed to meet our babies' needs, leading to improved parental sensitivity,[2] increased parental self-efficacy,[3] and enhanced child development outcomes.[4] Yet somehow, mindfulness tools to support us when we have small children are often overlooked.

Perhaps this is in part because most people with small children feel like they don't have a single extra brain cell to devote to anything new. That's why we developed the Nurture Method.

The Nurture Method is a revolutionary new way to approach mindfulness from an angle that makes it accessible when you're juggling all that small children can throw at you. Instead of trying to add one more thing to your day, we invite you to keep doing exactly what you're doing and simply use the principles of mindfulness to bring more joy, connection, and presence into your every day with baby. There's no magic to it. The Nurture Method sticks to the science of what works and gives you a different way of thinking about the same old things. With practical methods that are designed to meet you where you are, so can you set yourself up to be your best, respond as best you can to whatever life brings your way, and give yourself grace to recenter when things go wrong. By simply looking at things like diaper changes and playtime in a different light, you can love and appreciate more and fear and stress less.

The Nurture Method helps you to focus on the only two things you can control: how you prepare yourself and how you respond so that you can show up as best you can—responsive, interactive, present, and loving. Because in the end, that's the most important thing you and your baby need.

You got this!

How to Use This Book

The only way to use this book is the way that works for you.
This book is not intended to be read in a specific order or to be followed exactly. It's intended to have the information you need and to be easy for you to navigate to get the information you want.

Think of it like this: imagine this book is a big buffet loaded with dozens of dishes. What you put on your plate is entirely up to you. You might pile your plate high with just a few of your absolute favorite foods. You might do a mix of foods you love with a few new things you want to try. You might just sample everything at the table, taking one tiny piece from every dish. You might eat dessert first or have breakfast for dinner. You might create something entirely new by mixing things together. And don't forget about seconds! You can always come back for more when you're ready.

Treat this book like that giant buffet. There will be things shared here that you love, that you like, that you're not sure about, that you definitely don't want to do, that you want to explore later, and that you want to explore again and again. *You* get to build your own plate of mindfulness practices.

To help you, we've divided this book into three sections.

PART 1: MINDFULNESS AND THE NURTURE METHOD

Part 1 offers you the opportunity to dig into the roots of mindfulness and the Nurture Method itself. Don't worry, we keep it tired-parent-friendly as we explore what it means to be "mindful" and what concepts of mindfulness make up the Nurture Method. This section will help you understand the *why* of the techniques in part 2 and will allow you to begin to apply the Nurture Method in your own life, outside of the techniques we offer.

PART 2: TECHNIQUES

This is your hands-on section with step-by-step techniques that apply the Nurture Method in a variety of ways from play time to sleep time to me time. Each chapter is broken down into three sections to help you get to what you need quickly:

Overview: A quick summary of the chapter and how to apply the concepts of the Nurture Method to the specific topic.
How It Works: A brief look at the science, reasoning, and broader concepts around the technique.
Technique: Step-by-step instructions demonstrating some of the ways you can apply the Nurture Method to the concept, which you can begin implementing right away or use as inspiration to create your own techniques.

PART 3: INTEGRATING THE NURTURE METHOD

In part 3, you'll find practical components to help you integrate the Nurture Method into your day. Like anything new, success comes from starting small. We recommend little shifts, little changes. Small improvements consistently can make extraordinary outcomes. That's why it's an integration, not an overhaul. Part 3 is broken down into three sections:

Okay Now What: Our best practices for how to integrate the Nurture Method into your day.
The Nurture Method in Action: An overview of NEST (Nourish, Energize, Sleep, Tend), which is the Nurture Method daily rhythm. You'll find sample NEST days to give you an idea of how to create your

own version of NEST in different scenarios including: at home, at the hospital, and upon returning to work.
What to do when . . .: This is the emergency section with a list of some of the best go-to techniques for when you just need help now.

The Companion Workbook

Throughout the book, we will reference additional resources available in the companion workbook. You can download it at NurtureMethod.com. The free workbook gives you the chance to dive even deeper into the Nurture Method, putting the content into your hands. You will find reflection questions and mandala coloring pages for each chapter which we encourage you to use to process what you've read, as well as journaling pages, recommendation lists, and more.

Entering the Holy Order Not Required

Buddhism teaches that there are two paths you can follow: the monastic or the householder. Neither is better, both are needed in society, and *both* can find enlightenment—just in different ways and through different practices.

This is not a monastic book.

This is a book written *by* householders *for* householders. Rest assured, neither of the authors are living the perfect Zen life and accomplishing every single thing in this book with Instagram perfection. The methods shared here are meant to be used in a real and chaotic life. They are meant to be incorporated if and where they can. No robes or vow of silence required!

This is also not a religious or spiritual book.

Even though mindfulness practice can lean into the mystical, we have done our best to leave the mystical out of this book. We have focused on practical and, whenever possible, scientifically backed methods to help bring mental and emotional benefits to you and your family. That being said, we have *left room* for your beliefs and spirituality. If this book is a buffet, consider the faith element an optional topping. We will note some areas where you might want to incorporate your own beliefs, but remember that you are in charge and you can use this book any way that works for you.

Safety First

Nothing in this book should be taken as health or medical advice. We will share what we have learned, either from teachers or from our own personal experiences, but at the end of the day you should always consult with a medical professional before making any changes, and you should not use anything in this book as a substitute for medical care.

Meet Yourself Where You Are

No matter how you choose to use the Nurture Method, the key is to make it uniquely your own. Mindfulness means meeting yourself where you are, so we encourage you to engage with the content in a way that works for you. Let your fingers do the walking. Jump around, dog-ear pages, highlight, cross out, come back to whatever you want. Find the parts, and *only* the parts, that are supportive to you and use those. Or change them around until they become supportive. This is your book and only you get to decide what's best.

PART 1

MINDFULNESS AND THE NURTURE METHOD

1

Exploring Mindfulness

Before we can dive into the Nurture Method and how you can apply it to everyday mindfulness with your baby, we want to give you a parent-friendly overview of what we mean when we say "mindfulness" and how mindfulness applies to parenting. You might already be well versed in mindfulness or you might need some mindfulness techniques *this instant* to get you to a place where your brain has space to think about what mindfulness means. That's fine! You can skip this, you can skim this, you can come back to it later. Like everything in this book, it is only here to support you on your journey.

Now let's jump in!

Mindfulness is a buzzword these days. Literally. You can find articles on Buzzfeed about the best mindfulness products out there, the best mindfulness meditations under five minutes, and how to make a DIY mindfulness jar. But mindfulness isn't about apps that remind you to breathe or essential oils that help you relax, and it isn't about "me-time" or about getting Zen.

Mindfulness is your ability to perceive what is happening to and around you, *without getting caught up in it*, and make choices about how to respond based on your values.

Through the practice of mindfulness, you can teach your brain to recognize that the things you think and feel are temporary, and that none of those things are you or define you. That's not quite as fun or as marketable as a mindfulness coloring book, but it is a whole lot more powerful and useful.

The term "mindfulness" was coined in the 1970s, but the concepts have origins in practices, both religious and secular, that go back thousands of years, including Buddhism, Hinduism, Taoism, and Stoicism. These ancient practices teach us that our experiences are not us but are created moment-by-moment through three elements:

1) Your body feels through sensations. Your eyes see. Your ears hear. Your mouth tastes. Your nose smells. Your hands touch.
2) Your mind thinks through thoughts. Thoughts come and go (or stay if you let them) about new things, old things, and everything in between—but are often based on old patterns that tell you how you can be safe and comfortable.
3) Emotions are sparked by what you are sensing with your body and thinking with your mind. Emotions are energy in motion and meant to move through us.

None of these three things are bad. Quite the opposite, we need them in order to function in the world.

The problem comes in when we become consumed with them. Being too much in your *thoughts* can mean that you are not paying attention to what you are feeling and/or what your eyes see, hands touch, ears hear, and heart feels. Giving too much attention to what you are *feeling* causes you to lose awareness of what is happening around you, what you are thinking, and what your senses are taking in. Focusing too much on your *senses* takes you away from your internal experience of thoughts and feelings.

The things we experience can be all-consuming and it is easy, natural even, to have a thought, feeling, or emotion and think that it is you. But you are more.

You are the experiencer in the midst of the experience, the thinker who thinks the thought, the feeler who feels the emotion.

How can you connect with that observer part of yourself? Through mindfulness. Mindfulness is a practice that helps you become aware of all things that you are sensing, thinking, and feeling while also staying balanced and choosing how you respond to them.

Mindfulness creates space between what's coming up and how you choose to respond. So, when you experience something hard (as you always will, because life is hard and it only gets harder when you throw some kids into the mix!) you will not be instantly consumed by negative thoughts and feelings. Instead, you will be able to say, "Oh hey, I'm experiencing something hard right now and I'm thinking and feeling these things because of that." That simple realization will give you freedom and choices you didn't know you had before. Now you will be able to breathe. Pause. Accept. Extend compassion. Give yourself grace or whatever you need. Then you can return to the present moment, to make choices based on what your intentions are and be ready for the new experiences, new feelings, new thoughts that are just around the corner.

The practice of mindfulness helps you to be more aware of all the things going on in each moment and allows you to keep returning to that place of openness, curiosity, and nonjudgmental acceptance.

Let's break this down a little more.

Have you ever eaten a meal and realized that you emptied your plate without noticing a single bite? We often call that "autopilot," and it's a wonderful thing that our brains can do. Can you imagine if you had to really think through every action you took when you ate?

Okay, lift fork.
Stick into potato.
Insert food into mouth.
Open and close mouth.
Swallow.

How would you get through the day if you had to do that for every single thing? Thank God for autopilot, right?

The problem is that autopilot is not a perfect system. When autopilot is engaged, it leaves room for your mind to get busy thinking about all the things that minds like to think about: errands, grocery lists, that stupid thing your client said to you today, the party favors for your oldest's birthday, which paint color you want to choose for the living room, that embarrassing moment in eighth grade. And when your mind gets busy, you stop being aware of the present moment, of what you are experiencing, feeling, and what's going on around you. Again, sometimes that's good, sometimes we need to go onto autopilot so our brain can sort out other things. But when you're not in control of when autopilot gets turned on and off, you might not notice when it gets turned on.

For instance, if you're eating, you might not notice that the food is too hot. You might completely miss that there's a piece of bone in the mix. You might not enjoy a single bite of your favorite meal. And when you suffer the consequences of autopilot, you might find yourself left feeling disappointed, dissatisfied, even upset and frustrated.

Wow, I was looking forward to that meal all day, and I don't remember eating any of it.

Ugh I burned my tongue! That's going to suck for the rest of the day. I'm so mad.

Fortunately, and unfortunately, you can use autopilot in just about every area of your life. Your work, your hobbies, relationships, even taking care of a baby can be set to autopilot. And when that happens, you often arrive at your destination without knowing how you got there. You may get into a fight with your partner without being sure why things got so bad. You might reach the end of the day and have painfully tight shoulders for reasons you can't explain. You might get through a beautiful summer and realize you never savored a single second of the warm weather.

That is where mindfulness comes in.

Mindfulness lets autopilot do its job while allowing you to remain aware of what is going on inside of you (what you're thinking and feeling), focused on what is going on around you (what you're seeing and experiencing), and *conscious in your response*, even amid any chaos. That's a fancy way of saying that when you practice mindfulness, you may be on autopilot, but you're still the captain, still watching the controls, and still making real-time decisions about your flight.

This means you get the chance to be *proactive*, instead of *reactive*. Returning to the food analogy for a moment—mindfulness would help you pay attention to the food in front of you, so you could notice that the salad you ordered had strawberries in it so you don't end up spending the night covered in itchy rashes.

If you're thinking, "Mindfulness can't help prevent bad things from happening" then you would be absolutely correct! It can help us stay present, which can help us make choices to reduce hardship, but *mindfulness is not intended to make life easier*. Mindfulness is there to help us remain present and centered no matter what life throws at us.

So, let's see what that might look like. What happens if the strawberries were hidden in a vinaigrette and you didn't know? Or what happens if you were talking and just didn't notice? What happens if you are as mindful as possible and still *end up spending the night covered in itchy rashes?*

Remember we said that mindfulness was about *conscious response* even amid any chaos.

If being mindful meant that there would never be any errors, problems, discomfort, or mistakes, everyone would be practicing mindfulness and we would be living in utopia. As you're aware, we do not live in a utopia. No one has unlocked that secret.

But what has been unlocked is the ability to be okay when the errors, problems, discomforts, and mistakes happen. Through mindfulness, you can see the world more clearly and accept that what is happening is temporary. Because *everything is temporary*.

Here's how that might play out with Strawberry-gate.

Without mindfulness,

1) You lay in bed all night, miserable.
2) You're furious at yourself for not being more diligent and asking about strawberries.
3) The itching is driving you to tears, and it's pretty much all you can think about as you stare at the clock, which reads 2:00 a.m., aka the endless night.

With mindfulness,

1) You can see clearly that you are angry at yourself for not asking the server about strawberries in the meal. Instead of indulging those thoughts, which will only make you feel worse, you bring awareness to that thought, allow it to be, and then let it pass, knowing that you can learn from your mistake and that the anger you are feeling will dissipate.
2) Even though the rash is itchy as hell, you are aware that you are not your discomfort. Pain is only nerve receptors letting you know that something is amiss, and their messages do not define your entire reality. As the discomfort rolls through, you don't focus on the sensations, you breathe in and let it pass. You choose your response to what comes up to you and through you.
3) You can see the thoughts coming in, telling you that this discomfort will never end. You know it will though. Everything ends.

You watch those thoughts go by and allow them to pass, without pushing them down where they will only grow bigger and get clutched onto as eternal truths.

You still had to go through your terrible night, but with mindfulness, you were able to ride the waves instead of getting pulled under. You return to center, knowing ups and downs are a natural part of life.
Why is that?

When you come from a place of observation and acceptance, you begin to experience equanimity. Equanimity is the opposite of lying awake, miserable, angry, and hopeless. It is mental calmness, composure, and evenness of temper, especially in a difficult situation.

So now think about how that ability to observe, accept, and achieve equanimity could affect every area of your life through the power of mindfulness.

Instead of laying on your horn and feeling pissed off because you're stuck in traffic, you notice how the situation makes you feel and—instead of trying to fight the traffic or your feelings—accept both and know that they will pass.

Instead of spending the evening on the couch in a funk because you messed up on a report at work, you observe what you're experiencing and—rather than trying to make the mistake or the crappy feelings go away—you accept both and know neither will last forever.

Instead of snapping at your partner because they left their socks on the floor *again*, you observe your reaction and—rather than trying to control your partner or your feelings—you accept that both the situation and the feelings will pass and there will be an opportunity for you two to talk it out.

None of this is easy. And none of it is a permanent state of being. You don't just become mindful and stay there. It's a practice. The more you practice being there, the easier it becomes. The more you are able to recognize when you are not in this state, the more you are able to pause, recenter, and get back there.

Now that you understand how powerful mindfulness can be, can you think of a better tool in your childcare toolbox? How often do you need equanimity when dealing with your little ones? How often do you live on autopilot with them, reacting to things without ever being aware of what you're doing? If you're anything like us, the answer is pretty much all the time. We'll talk a little bit more about mindfulness and babies below but first, let's take a look at the root of mindfulness: meditation.

MINDFULNESS AT ITS CORE: MEDITATION

Now we've taken a broad look at what mindfulness is: awareness and conscious response. We've talked about how mindfulness brings equanimity through the ability to watch our internal and external experiences and to accept them without judgement.

Let's take one more step and zoom in close to see what that looks like in its purest form: meditation. *Meditation is the foundation out of which mindfulness is built.* Through the practice of meditation, you learn how to experience your thoughts, feelings, and sensations without getting attached to them. Meditation teaches you how to observe your thoughts as they come and then let them go.

There's more to meditation than just sitting in silence. You don't need to go to an ashram to practice meditation, and you don't need to be a guru (or a bendy Instagram yogi, for that matter) to practice meditation. Meditation is an everyday practice for everyday people. Yes, it can be done in silence. But it can also be done on the go, while you're walking, or driving, or even talking. Meditation, like mindfulness, isn't about some mystical state of supreme awakening. It's simply about training your brain to become aware of your thoughts, feelings, and senses and to have the equanimity to make choices based on your values rather than your reactions.

The best way to learn about meditation is to try it, so we've compiled some parent tested and approved meditation practices. Maybe you've tried meditation before or maybe this is your first time learning more about it. No matter where you fall on the meditation spectrum, we'd like to invite you to try one or more of these, "I have kids and I can't spend hours finding Nirvana" meditations as a way to learn more about mindfulness.

Your first instinct may be to skip over this part. Don't do it! If you want to get the most out of this book, it's important to truly experience the core of what you're working toward.

Here's what we recommend: select a practice below and do it for five minutes a day for one week. Five minutes! You got this. And we're going to help you. Start by reading through the techniques below and choosing the one you'd like to try first.

TECHNIQUES TO PRACTICE MINDFULNESS

Focused Breath

This is perhaps the simplest way to meditate because you are just bringing awareness and attention to your breath. You can do it as you walk, when you are waiting in line, or as you feed your little one. You can breathe normally or use any of the breathing techniques we cover in chapter 6.

- Bring your awareness and attention to your breath
- Notice the rising and falling of your chest and belly as you breathe in and out
- Feel the sensation of the air moving in and out of your body
- When your mind wanders, gently bring your attention back to your breath
- Focus on the constant rhythmic motion of your breath, connecting your mind, body, and soul
- With each mindful breath, feel yourself reset and recenter, cultivating a sense of calm and clarity in the present moment

Body Scan

This technique helps you connect with your body from head to toe as you do focused breathing. This is a great practice to do before you go to sleep or when you wake up. But it works just as well in traffic or the waiting room at the doctor's office.

- Begin by focusing on your feet. Take a moment to think about all that your feet do for you. They may not be perfect, they may hurt sometimes, but they are the foundation of your being and they carry you each day, providing stability and balance. Picture all the places your feet have taken you in your life or in the last few minutes.

- Breathe in and send gentle loving awareness to your feet which ground you, and give thanks for them.
- Breathe out and move up from your feet to your legs.
- Breathe in and think about how amazing your legs are. They carry the weight of your body, allowing you to walk, run, and dance. Picture all the ways your legs have helped you today—from carrying your little one to holding you up during a long day.
- Breath out and extend gentle loving awareness to your legs which support you, and give thanks for them.
- Continue with each area of your body, stomach, chest/heart, arms and hands, neck, mouth, ears, nose, eyes, and finally the crown of your head. You can even affirm something like, "I am whole, perfect and complete from the crown of my head to the soles of my feet."
- As you do this scan, you can notice any areas on your body where you feel discomfort. Your goal is to bring awareness along with a nonjudgmental curiosity as you scan your whole body.

Labeling and Noting

Labeling helps train your mind to focus on what you are experiencing now in this moment, instead of worrying or ruminating about the past or future. Practicing this kind of awareness in non-stressful situations will help you be more aware and mindful in situations that are more stressful or challenging. Labeling is a meditation practice you can utilize anytime, anywhere—cooking, driving, eating, and even playing!

- Wherever you are, begin to label whatever you are experiencing with your senses in the moment.
- Go through each of the five senses. For example, if you are waiting at a traffic light, you might say, "I hear the blare of the police siren. I see the bright red traffic light. I feel the rumble of car engine. I smell my baby's dirty diaper. I feel tired."

    If you are walking down the street, you might say, "I see the tree. I hear the hum of the train. I taste cool air. I smell bread from the bakery across the street. I feel my mittens on my fingers. I feel tightness in my knee."
- Don't judge or try to change what you label, simply note it.

Loving-Kindness

Within all of us is the ability to be loving and kind. It's often easier to extend loving-kindness to another who is suffering than to one's own self. Think about that twinge of heart within you when you see someone else suffering. You feel the desire to help; you feel compassion for them. You can practice this and intentionally extend loving kindness to yourself and others. When you are suffering, feeling negativity, guilt, or shame, you can use this practice to return to love and find peace.

- Think about someone you love (it could be a pet, a child, a friend)—someone who is easy for you to love.
- See them in your mind's eye and say, "May you feel love, may you feel peace, may you feel loving-kindness."
- Now think of someone else—someone you struggle to love at times.
- Think of them in your mind's eye and say, "May you feel love, may you feel peace, may you feel loving-kindness."
- Lastly, think about yourself, and know that at any time, you can extend the same loving-kindness to yourself that you extended to others. Put your hand on your heart and say, "May I feel love, may I feel peace, may I feel loving-kindness."

Visualization

Visualization is about the future which, at first glance, may not seem like it will help you become more centered in the here and now. But in actuality, meditating on the future you desire to see will help you stay focused in the present so you can make choices that align with your goals instead of merely doing what is easier. Once you understand where you are going, you will find yourself excited about the creation of it day by day.

- As you begin or end your day, while brushing your teeth, taking your thirty-second shower, or putting baby to bed, visualize the next few hours going exactly as you desire them to.
- Mentally step through your routine and the various activities you have planned, and see yourself moving through them easily and joyfully.

- Imagine: How do you feel, what are you doing, who surrounds you, and what does it look like? Remember to allow other people and external situations to be as they are, and focus only on your experience and how you are feeling, since that's all we can control.
- If you journal, make some notes about what you see unfolding in your ideal vision for today, tomorrow, or into the future.
- You can do this exercise for envisioning even further into your future. Allow yourself to visualize what you want in your life across all different areas (health/wellness, wealth/work, love/relationships, happiness/joy, and your home/energy) and really feel what it would feel like to realize your vision across all these important areas.

Appreciation

When we want the moment in front of us to be different than what it is we are no longer in the present. We are in our heads, imagining how it *should* be. The Appreciation meditation trains our brains to find happiness in the present moment because there is always something (usually lots of things!) to appreciate right now.

- Bring to mind something in the present moment that you can appreciate, no matter how small it may seem (e.g., the sound of your baby's gentle breathing, your body that is able to care for them, the cup of coffee that is going to keep you functional).
- Reflect on why you appreciate this moment, how it fills your heart with love, and how it makes you feel grateful.
- Expand your appreciation to other aspects of your life. It can be about your little one—like the simple joys of parenthood or the support of your partner or family member—but it doesn't have to be. You can appreciate your friends, your career, or yes even yourself! Think about your strengths, health, and achievements!
- Take a few deep breaths and let the sense of gratitude sink in, noticing where you feel it in your body.

Reflection

Taking some time to reflect after meditation is a powerful practice. You can do this either by writing down what came up or just taking a moment to look back on your experience and how it made you feel. This is especially useful as you try different techniques so you get a sense of what feels best for you.

Here are some questions to ask yourself after a meditation session. You can think through the answers or if it's helpful, you can download the companion workbook at NurtureMethod.com where you can print and write down your answers.

- When I meditate, do I notice when my thoughts or feelings distract me from my practice?
- Do I make judgments about my meditation experience? If it was "good" or "bad" or what came up for me?
- How do I feel after meditation? Any different?
- Has meditation taught me anything about myself or how I experience myself?
- Are there times during the day where I can use what I practiced in meditation to help me in the moment?
- How do I feel later on in the day after I meditated? (Oftentimes the actual meditation will be uncomfortable, but you'll feel more centered later in the day and find yourself to not be as reactive to situations that are out of your control.)

No matter what your answers are, even if you got nothing out of your practice—don't judge yourself. It is all part of the process. And it is only the beginning. Once you start to learn about meditation, you can find what works best for you. These meditations are only a small sample of the many incredible ways to explore this practice.

Make a Meditation Commitment

Once you've selected the meditation you want to try, make a commitment to do five minutes a day for a week. One week will give you enough time to explore the practice and begin to experience some of the benefits.

Don't worry if that feels like too much. If, how, and when you do it is entirely up to you! And it's not necessary in order to start using the Nurture Method. But if you want to try it out, we have a tool to help you accomplish it. Did you know one of the best ways to make a commitment to a goal is to create a contract with yourself and sign it?[1] Yes, science has again backed up a mindfulness concept and shown that when you set an intention, it can help you achieve it. So, in the companion workbook at NurtureMethod.com we have put together a meditation contract. When you're ready, *if* you're ready, to make a commitment to do five minutes of judgment-free, stress-free, not kid-free, meditation every day, then fill out the contract. We recommend you print it out and put it somewhere highly visible, like your bathroom mirror or your phone lock screen to remind yourself to take those five minutes for yourself.

MAKE IT A HABIT

While not a requirement, it can be helpful to choose a specific time to meditate each day. By consistently meditating at the same time, the practice becomes a habit, a seamless part of your day, rather than a last-minute-oh-shoot-did-I-meditate-today experience. There are apps that will remind you to meditate throughout the day or you can simply set an alarm on your phone.

MINDFULNESS FOR YOU AND BABY—PLANTING THE SEED

After reading through the ins and outs of mindfulness and meditation, you've got to be wondering how any of that applies to a baby. Babies aren't going to meditate and are pretty much *only* aware of the present moment. So what's the point of all of this? Excellent question.

We're going to answer that question, but only if you promise one thing: don't get caught up in thinking your every move is going to make or break your child. The fact that you are the kind of person who is reading this book should assure you what a wonderful caregiver you are. You want to give your baby the best—and you are already doing that, simply by the depth of your love and caring.

So now, with that in mind, let's talk about what it means to teach your baby mindfulness. Just to be clear, after applying the concepts of this book you will not walk into your nursery one day and find your baby seated in meditation. In the same way that when you play music for your baby, it's not with the intention of turning them into a musical prodigy, or you when read to them, it's not with the intention of turning them into a great novelist, you can bring mindfulness to your little one as a way to plant the seeds of a way of being that will support them, entertain them, and engage them—without the intention of turning them into a Zen master.

We're going to cover three ways that mindfulness practices can help your baby both now and in the future (this is the part where you have to keep your promise to not overthink!).

Happy You Means a Happy Baby

We've talked about how the practice of mindfulness brings heightened levels of well-being, happiness, patience, acceptance, and compassion to adults. Well, guess who else benefits from that? Yep! Your baby does—babies are intuitive little beings and from day one, they are paying attention to your emotions. According to Jennifer E. Lansford, PhD, a professor with the Social Science Research Institute and the Center for Child and Family Policy at Duke University, "Because your child uses you as a gauge for emotional cues and reactions, they're attuned to your emotions, even if you don't realize it. From birth, infants pick up on emotional cues from others." They aren't just attuned to our emotions, they learn from them too, Dr. Lansford said. "Even very young infants look to caregivers to determine how to react to a given situation."[2]

Nowadays, with our phones demanding our attention, our email never stopping, the twenty-four-hour news cycle, and the expectation that we can get it all done and then some, our autopilots are always engaged. You rarely get time to be still and connect with the present moment and with your own self. And your little one notices this. When you learn to stay centered and find joy in life, even in the face of life's inevitable stressors—and with an infant you will have many—you are modeling for your baby how to be wholehearted and happy. And that happiness will last a lifetime! Literally. A twenty-nine-year study found that happier babies are not only more successful, they're also just plain happier as adults![3]

This dynamic poses a great responsibility for parents. A responsibility that is best met by turning within. Within is where you find the answers for how to meet your child's needs. Your child is like no other who has ever been or ever will be, just as you are like no one else or ever will be. You are unique—made up of your own experiences, drive, and gifts—and so is each of your babies. Using the tools of mindfulness in your own life allows you to connect with your baby and better understand what they need moment to moment. More than anything, it's your loving presence that your baby needs and being present is how you can enjoy the love your baby brings and better handle the confusion, frustration, and bewilderment that comes along with that love. When you are in a mindful state, you're better able to bring what is needed to a situation, whether it be patience, calm, empathy, or love—and this is more impactful for your baby than any piece of expert advice.

Habits Start Now

Babies start trying to make sense of their world the moment they come into it. And research tells us that a newborn *immediately* starts to take note of repeated behaviors and prepares to imitate them. That shouldn't come as too much of a surprise—think about it, after just a few weeks, our babies smile at us when we smile at them. By a few months, they begin to recognize words and coo back at us when we speak to them. We often say that babies are sponges, but they're also like mirrors, taking in what is around them and reflecting it back.

What that means is now, right now, you can begin to create the foundation of supportive habits for your children. According to First Things First,[4] "starting from birth, children develop brain connections through their everyday experiences. A young child's daily experiences determine which brain connections develop and which will last for a lifetime. The amount and quality of care, stimulation and interaction they receive in their early years makes all the difference." From day one, they can experience the mindfulness habits that come from everyday activities like the bliss of song and the power of mantra, the comfort of rituals and the bond of storytelling.

When you begin forming those habits today, you create the riverbed for the water to flow through. As they mature, your children will be ready to start their own mindfulness practice, if they so choose, because the habits will already be there. It will be the difference between learning a new language as an adult and picking up a language that is already familiar to them.

Nature vs. Nurture

Your baby's nature is unique. But the beauty of mindfulness lies in its ability to meet your child *exactly where they are*, and Nurture them in their own special way. By practicing mindfulness with them from the beginning, you create an environment that nurtures their nature. And as parents, that's the best we can hope for. Because while we can plant seeds in our children, we can't make the sun rise or the rain fall or the seed sprout. What we *can* do—what this whole meditation and mindfulness thing is about and what this whole book is about—is apply the practices in our own life and seek equanimity for ourselves. When we do this, we invite our little ones to become who they were meant to be and then release the outcome without judgement, entrusting them to find their own way to blossom, and making room for growth, connection, and joy in the journey. Because, in the end, it's all about the journey.

2

The Nurture Method

Now that you understand the basics of mindfulness, of watching your internal and external experiences without judgment and making conscious choices, do you think you can explain that to your newborn baby?

Obviously not.

In fact, you've probably already realized that your baby is better at mindfulness than you are! Without a past to help them define what they are experiencing or any concept of the future to worry about, everything simply *is*. They may cry because they have a wet diaper but not because they feel shame about wetting their diaper or because they're feeling overwhelmed with all the steps to get a new one. They're crying because their diaper is wet. Change the diaper, and the problem is solved. It's as if it never happened, because if you really think about it—to them, it didn't. There is only now. The past is gone, and they don't grasp the future yet.

However, as you have seen or will see all too soon, that total freedom from past and future is short-lived. Little ones quickly start to build narratives about the world, about how things were or how they should be. It's a perfectly natural and necessary skill—we as humans must be able to learn from the past and use that information to prepare for the future in order to survive! As we discussed, the problem with that skill comes when you get stuck in the past and the future and miss your present. That's where mindfulness comes in, providing you with the tools to get grounded in the present moment and experience life as it is, not through the lens of your narratives.

Now, we said you can't explain mindfulness to a baby. But can you *teach* a baby mindfulness?

That's a big, resounding yes.

Why? Because babies are always watching and learning, and while you can't explain concepts, you *can* teach through actions and behaviors that will lay a foundation for what is to come.

Sounds great, right? Sure, probably for celebrities who have time because their personal chef, live-in nanny, and cleaning staff give them the free time to be super-parents and look good while they're at it. For the rest of us, who can barely remember to brush our teeth, what are we supposed to do?

No, really, *what on earth* are we supposed to do?

This was a question we posed to each other on a frosty winter day. As mindfulness practitioners and educators and as mothers, we wanted to know if there was something else out there for parents besides Mommy and Me yoga, something that could help us connect with our mindfulness practices, stay supported in the moment, but also be, well, doable. We started looking at what mindfulness resources were available for new parents and after a while, we both had arrived at the same conclusion: there didn't seem to be any of those resources. Was it because what we were talking about was impossible? We didn't think so. *There had to be a way to take the concepts of mindfulness, distill them into something actionable, and infuse them into everyday life in a way that is actually manageable for real people, even people with babies—especially people with babies.*

We began to explore. Through our studies, our work, and our experiences, we sought to understand the practice of mindfulness through the eyes of a child.

What we found were three core ingredients of mindfulness that kept coming up over and over:

1. Stillness: It takes many forms, from silence to physical rest, but it always involves slowing down and allowing our bodies to experience the present moment.
2. Observation: The simple act of noticing what is around you, what you are thinking, and what you are feeling.
3. Intention: Choosing deliberately, rather than making decisions dictated by habit or expectation.

Separated into three concrete and simple actions, it suddenly didn't feel so overwhelming. And we found ourselves asking the big question: *what if we applied those three concepts to everyday life with our babies?*

ENTER: THE NURTURE METHOD

As we began to explore and eventually teach this method, what we found was that mindfulness with babies was not only possible, it was also simple and *Nurturing* to both parents and their babies!

The Nurture Method is a new way of approaching mindfulness. It invites you, with your hands full of kiddos and toys and your brain full of lists and sleepless nights, to let go of trying to add one more thing to your day and instead sprinkle the concepts of stillness, observation, and intention into whatever you are *already doing*. Stinky diaper changes? Yes. Late night rocking sessions? Yes. Messy meal time? Yes. Sibling play time? Yes, yes, and yes! When core elements of mindfulness become a spice you can sprinkle onto anything you do, the possibilities are endless! And what we found, and we're sure you will too, is that incorporating these three things into your everyday life will help you create an environment that allows you and your children to flourish.

The Nuture Method recipe.

Let's explore these three concepts in more depth and see what it means to apply them to everyday life. Just like the Nurture Method is meant to help you plant the seeds of mindfulness in your child, the information and activities we explore below are meant to plant the seeds of the Nurture Method concepts. Don't get overwhelmed trying to understand it all and do all the activities we cover. You can jump straight into the techniques but if you want to understand the ideas behind them so you can begin to apply them in other areas of your life, keep reading. If you don't have the time or energy to study it all, that's okay. You might be surprised at what takes root and how these concepts will come back to you later!

1. STILLNESS

In the previous chapter, we looked at meditation and provided some easy meditations for you to try out. You may notice that none of them required complete and utter silence. Silence and *stillness* are often conflated, but in fact they are two very different things.

Silence is practically impossible. Try playing a round of "who can stay silent the longest" with your children, and you will see just how hard it is. Even if you do somehow find yourself in total silence, whatever that means, your body will never be silent. Your heart will beat, your lungs breathe, your cells divide, and as we discussed, your brain will think.

With mindfulness, *silence* is not the goal. Silence is the absence of noise, but stillness is a state of being. Picture, if you will, a large lake that is completely still. When you think of a still lake, do you think of a lake that is frozen over, motionless and lifeless? Or do you picture a gentle body of water that is quiet, with water slowly lapping on the beach, dimpled by fish surfacing for lunch, and sparkling in the warm sun?

Stillness is a foundational practice of mindfulness and meditation because it helps us become that still lake, very much in motion, very much teeming with life, but so calm that the passing clouds can reflect in its cool surface. Yes, the storms will rage and the boats will zoom through and the children will cannonball into the calmness. But as we become more and more present in the moment through our practices, we have the ability to return to that place of calm quickly instead of being overtaken by what is happening around us and inside us.

Of course, that is not to say that silence has nothing to do with the stillness of mindfulness. Yes, you can achieve stillness inside, even on the busiest playground. But part of growing still *is* growing quiet. It is in the quiet moments that our minds can truly get focused and centered on what is happening right now, in the present moment. In the Bible, we are told, "Be still and know that I am God" (Psalm 46:10), which is a beautiful practice in mindfulness and meditation. It doesn't say, "Go to the very back of the darkest cave, and only there in the deepest, blackest, silence will you know Me." It says, "Shhhh. If you want to know and be known, you have to grow still and listen."

Love, beauty, and peace wait in the stillness that is within us. We just need to slow down enough to hear it.

Children and Stillness

We don't like stillness. We find it awkward. We find it uncomfortable. We try to fill it. Think about the last time you were intentionally quiet. When was the last time you turned off the television or took out your headphones and allowed your thoughts to be your only company and entertainment? When was the last time you sat quietly beside someone without talking? When was the last time you worked or cleaned without music? Can't remember? Most people can't, and that's because most of us suffer from noise addiction. Overexposure to noise can be as addictive as a chemical substance, and when we become addicted, we suffer withdrawal without it.[1]

Businesses love addictions. They keep us coming back for more. So of course, they're eager to support our noise habit. If we always *need* noise, then we will always need *them* to provide us with music and television and podcasts and movies that create the noise. And, bonus for them, when they create those things, they get to fill them with advertising to remind us of all the other things they provide that we need.

In stillness, we take our power back. We become self-reliant. We become more comfortable with ourselves. We become more *present*. Are you beginning to see how this all ties together?

This training to fear stillness starts early with our children. One stroll down the baby aisle or one scroll through the top toys of the year and you'll be hard pressed to find anything that doesn't come fully loaded with a barrage of colors, images, lights, sounds, and movement. Obviously the loudest, brightest, flashiest thing will always grab our attention, but does that mean it's what we need? The marketing industry for children sure wants you to think so. They're counting on it.

The Science of Stillness

As we mentioned, "stillness" and "silence" are often used interchangeably, even though they mean different things, especially when it comes to the practice of mindfulness. The scientific community has begun studying "silence" which, if you read through the studies, you will see is closer to our description of stillness then utter silence. Once again, what our wise teachers through the ages have been telling us is now backed by science. Turns out, quiet and stillness are an important part of your child's development—and the side benefit is that you'll get something out of it too. Here are just a few of the physical benefits from getting quiet:

- It makes our brains grow: a 2013 study found that quiet developed new brain cells.[2] That seems like something that would be especially important for growing minds, doesn't it?
- It lets our brain process: When we eliminate auditory distraction, our brains are better able to handle the information we take in. For a baby who constantly takes in new information, this is key!
- It reduces stress: Can babies be stressed? You bet they can. One study found that babies who regularly experience the stress hormone cortisol can develop physical and emotional problems down the road.[3] But quiet is one way to combat that. Another study found that stillness can relieve tension in the body and brain, even more so than listening to music![4]

The Art of Stillness

But there are more than just scientific benefits. There are emotional and mental benefits that come with getting still and quiet. And this is where things get really juicy. When we allow our children to experience silence during an activity, we leave room for:

- Concentration
- Imagination
- Creativity
- Boredom
- Frustration
- Disinterest
- Reengagement
- Solution
- Connection
- Exploration
- Gentleness

You probably noticed there are "positive" and "negative" words in that list. At first glance, things like frustration, disinterest, boredom may not seem as great as exploration, imagination, or concentration. But mindfulness teaches us to throw away those labels and instead focus on what is happening, instead of what we're feeling. Today, we're encouraged to shy away from "negative" feelings. And in our children, at the first sign of their displeasure, we often react quickly to try to fix the problem. But actually, those "negative" responses have positive outcomes. Discomfort is an important part of the learning process, and it creates resilience for the inevitable challenges that will come throughout life. When your child experiences frustration, it gives them a chance to search for a solution. When they feel disinterested or bored, it's an opportunity for them to discover something new that they enjoy.

Ways to Explore Stillness in Your Life:

- *Media-free Monday:* choose one day a week (Mondays make a lovely alliteration, but you can pick any day) when you will choose not to turn on entertainment for yourself. That means no music, no podcasts, no TV, no radio.
- *Commute in quiet:* it's hard to find quiet at work and home, but there is that precious time to and from work (or the grocery store or daycare) when you can choose silence.

- *Wake up to silence:* when you wake up, do you immediately grab your phone? Put the phone down and soak up the silence. Don't close your eyes and fall back asleep (that's called snoozing). Keep your eyes open but choose stillness. Take some deep breaths (the breathing techniques in chapter 6 work just as well on you as they do on baby!) and be in the moment, in the quiet.
- *Seize the in-between times:* Your baby is down for a nap. They're playing in their play yard. Grandma has just come by to pick them up. It's hard not to pop in your earbuds and get to work or to flop on the couch, turn on the TV, and catch some well-deserved R&R. Both of those are great. But before you do, grab a moment for silence. You don't need to pop into lotus and do a two-hour meditation. But sit still (or stand or, sure, do lotus) for just a minute, close your eyes, and give your mind a moment of stillness.
- *Nature:* Going for a walk in nature is best, but even just looking at scenic pictures or listening to a nature soundtrack can help you get still. There is a natural stillness in the natural world. Making some time in your day to be in nature, to observe, explore, and reflect allows you to tune into that stillness and natural flow that is within you too.
- *Create a practice:* Practice is a fancy word for "routine," and you've probably already got a lot of those with your baby. Why not create one for yourself? It could be a few quiet stretches every morning or a couple of minutes watching the sunset without any talking or music. Maybe it's good old-fashioned meditation before bed. Find what works for you and turn it into something that you can practice daily.

Incorporate Stillness into Your Day-to-Day with Baby

As you begin to seek out ways to find stillness, you will find it easier and easier to incorporate it into your interactions with your baby. Much of what you do by yourself, you will be able to do with your child as well. We'll cover these in depth in the "Technique" chapters, but here are some broad strokes to get you thinking about what sprinkling stillness into your day could look like:

- *Play:* When playing with your child, make sure that you include blocks of time where there is no noise and no distractions. *Pause* and give them time to take in whatever they are doing. Taking it in doesn't mean that they stare deeply into your eyes and nod knowingly. They might look away and focus on something else entirely. That's okay! Remember that quiet gives them time to process information.
- *Reading:* When you turn a page, don't just start reading. Instead, each time, first pause and be silent. Allow your baby the chance to look at the pictures and feel the pages. When you're done reading, give one more pause to take in everything you just said.
- *Talking:* When you talk to your baby, leave some space after you speak. You might be surprised to find that if you give them enough time to think, they will respond to you! Turns out, your silence can help build their vocabulary!
- *Singing:* Have some favorite tunes you love to sing with your baby? Hold a silence between verses and take a few breaths. Let your baby enjoy the fun of the music they just heard before starting more. Or have some fun with silence and leave out a few words. Just like talking to your baby and waiting for an answer, singing a familiar song and dropping the last part can help your baby learn and grow. The quiet gives them that opportunity to fill in the information you're leaving out. Even if they can't sing along just yet, it doesn't mean that their little brains aren't doing the work or that they won't gurgle at you to try anyway!
- *Being present:* No talking, no singing, no playing, no reading. Simply be. In the silence, you are afforded the opportunity to be together without distraction. Look into your baby's eyes (another important activity for babies that helps their brains tune in and learn) and let them gaze back into yours. Smile, connect, share your love. Study their beautiful face and let them study yours. Watch what catches their attention in the silence, see it with them, and then be ready for them when they return to look at you again. These are moments you will never regret having with your baby.

Phone Silence Is Not Mindful Quiet

Staring at your phone may make you still and quiet, but it is not the type of stillness or quiet we are striving for. Notice that the activities listed above all involve engaging with your baby in stillness. When planting the seeds of mindfulness with your baby, use stillness as a tool to be together with them, not as an opportunity to be distracted and do something else.

2. OBSERVATION

Our minds are constantly thinking, replaying thoughts, beliefs, and memories like an old cassette tape. We've all laid awake at night remembering that hurtful thing someone said in high school or worrying about how the meeting will go tomorrow. When you think about those things, about something that happened in the past or might happen in the future, you experience feelings with them too. Perhaps sadness, anger, shame, anxiety. But these kinds of thoughts don't only happen at night. They're always there, operating beneath our conscious awareness. Our brain is always processing the world using the past and future as a guide and stirring up feelings about what was, what should be, or what might be.

When we let these thoughts run unchecked, when we don't observe them, we can begin to react to the world in our head instead of the world in front of us. Mindfulness invites us to become observers. To see the world, and our thoughts, without judgment, allowing our experiences to come and go without getting entangled. As observers, we can learn to notice what is happening around us without becoming identified with it, which allows us to be intentional in our response instead of reactionary.

The Benefits of Observation

As we cultivate the ability to observe, we become more open and accepting of what is happening around us because we find that we're only responsible for our responses, not the emotions or actions of others (not even our children!). We see our baby and those around us as unique individuals, each with their own feelings and experiences. This awareness allows us to be more patient, compassionate, and understanding and to be able to show up with curiosity, openness, and excitement, sharing in our baby's experiences and joys. And yes, that's backed by science. Studies have shown that mindful observation can decrease the brain's default mode network, which is responsible for rumination and worry,[5] *and* increase the production of neurotransmitters such as dopamine and serotonin, which play a crucial role in mood regulation and emotional well-being![6]

But being able to observe without judgment also allows us to face the challenges that life presents us. Research has shown that observing our thoughts and the world around us without judgment literally can alter the structure and function of our brains, leading to increased gray matter in areas related to attention, emotion regulation, and memory![7] This process, known as neuroplasticity, lets our brains adapt and change in response to new experiences and environments. That means when new situations arise, our brains have the flexibility to handle it. And we suddenly have room in our minds to ask things like, "What choices do I want to make? What can I learn from this experience? How can I grow and heal from old patterns?" With this amazing new ability, we can find meaning in challenges and appreciate the lessons learned and we can begin to see that even the hard things have value, and we can grow from them.

Ways to Explore Observation in Your Own Life

Observing your own triggers

As we mentioned before, your mind will always be thinking, your heart will always be feeling, your body will be sensing and experiencing. Your work is being aware of all those things that are coming up.

As you become more aware, you are able to create some space between what happens and how you choose to respond. This gentle awareness and space allow you to be in flow without getting caught up in it all. To find peace in your heart even when it's chaotic outside.

Your brain's #1 job is to keep you alive and safe. That's what a trigger is: your brain's way of telling you *we've done this before and it's not safe! Engage safety measures that have worked before!*

Observation begins with curiosity. Start to get curious when you have a strong reaction to something. When you feel angry, frustrated, excited, sad, bored, lonely—either during or afterward—take a moment to get curious. Ask yourself:

- What caused the reaction?
- What was the story I told myself about what was going on?

- Was it a familiar story?
- What did it feel like in my body?
- How did my breath change?
- Did my posture or body language change?
- What is the intensity of this emotion?
- How long did it last?
- Did it shift or change over time?

Observe If Your Own Thoughts Are Serving You

It is estimated that humans have something close to 60,000 thoughts a day, and the majority of them are the same thoughts you had yesterday.[8] Not only are most of your thoughts repetitive, but a large chunk of them also are negative.[9] So, if we think negative things over and over and over again, our brains build connections that send us down those negative patterns and pathways without, well, thinking about it.

Through observation, you can retrain your brain to be aware of those repetitive thoughts. Observation lets us look at those thought patterns that may have been unconsciously directing us and begin to ask the question: are those pathways and patterns serving us? If not, we now have the choice to create new, positive pathways.

Once you become better at observing your thoughts and feelings, now you can start to explore them. You might begin to ask yourself questions like:

- Are these reactions based on facts or assumptions?
- Are these reactions helping me or holding me back?
- Are there any patterns or themes in my reactions?
- Are my reactions aligned with my values and goals?
- What would I say to a friend in this situation?
- What's the opportunity in this situation?
- What can I learn from this experience?

As you become able to observe what you are experiencing in the world around you, you can begin to have a new kind of freedom. The freedom to find your flow and in turn, connect with your baby. This presence makes your baby feel calm and safe and loved and creates patterns and pathways for how they see the world.

Observing Your Baby's Discomfort

From babies' earliest moments, they feel discomfort, be it hunger, tiredness, or feeling cold. Their discomfort grows into your discomfort. Sometimes you don't know what they need or you know and can't give them what they need, and you may become stressed in response. It's in these moments that you can use your new skill of observation. By observing what you see and feel, you will be better able to understand, respond to, and meet their needs. For many of us, babies who are uncomfortable can trigger all sorts of narratives and feelings. Perhaps you feel helpless and may start to think you are not able to care for them the way you should. Maybe you feel angry and your brain writes a narrative about how nothing you do is good enough. Perhaps you remember how your parents weren't able to care for you and you start to feel desperate to ensure your baby never feels that way.

But those thoughts won't serve you and they certainly won't serve your little one.

We may want to take away any discomfort for our littles, but it's not our job to ensure they live without any discomfort. How would they grow? Learn resilience? Learn to persevere?

Discomfort is part of the process—ours and theirs. Little ones have so much to learn and they have the ability to keep going, even when it's hard. It's innate. You see this drive when babies learn to walk. They fall and try again. Fall and try again. We can't do this for them, but we can be there with them and the best way to do that is by observing your reactions and choosing to remain present. Remembering that your loving presence is the best support you can give them is important. They must lean into discomfort to grow, just as you do. Because as babies grow into toddlers and toddlers grow into school-age and beyond—discomforts continue and feelings just get bigger and more complicated. You can never fight fire with fire. Your calm and observing presence is the best way to help them move through the tough things they will inevitably face.

3. INTENTION

Intention is at the crux of mindfulness. It is one step of the Buddha's eightfold path and it is said that he taught that everything "rests on the tip of intention."

As usual, science has gone on to prove what the ancients discovered long ago. For instance, in 2010, a researcher studied 106 students who were learning French as a second language.[10] Half, or 53 of them, were taught in the conventional fashion and the other 53 were given explicit instructions on *how to listen*. The result was that the latter group "significantly outperformed" the former. What does this have to do with intention? Everything! It shows that when people approach a situation with a specific set of instructions, or an *intention*, they are more likely to achieve their goal. In this case, the students who knew what to listen for were able to get more of what they wanted. And when it comes to your own life, the same is true. When you approach your life with intention, when you know what it is you are seeking, you are more likely to find it (that's why we gave you a contract to sign for your meditation goal).

Life, unfortunately, isn't as simple as a French test. The answers aren't usually a binary right or wrong, and that becomes even more true when a baby comes into the picture. But that doesn't mean that intention isn't a useful or important tool. In fact, setting your intention becomes more important when your world becomes more chaotic. Here's another way to think of it. Your day will be busy, guaranteed. Especially once that little one arrives. But *in order to make it less busy and more full of things that you like and that bring you joy, you have to be intentional.* Otherwise, it quickly fills up with all sorts of things that others want of you.

Intention setting is about picking a direction, setting your compass, and following it. If you've ever hiked using a compass, you know that your path is never a perfectly straight line. You have to alter your course to navigate around trees, rocks, rivers, and whatever else the landscape throws at you. You may have to go off course to avoid the wasp nest you spotted or you might go out of your way to find a nice clearing to set up your tent or take a long break, soaking your feet in a cool pond. Even still, your destination never changes. You always look to your compass and continue heading in the right direction.

It's important to understand that setting an intention is not the same as setting a goal. Like that French test, a goal is binary. Either you achieve it or you don't. However, intention is not about some future achievement, it is about your present. When you act with intention, you choose to live your values in *this* moment. You cannot control the future, you can't control who your children will become, you can't even control your own heartbeat. But you can control what you do in the only moment you have, the one right now. Intentions are not New Year's resolutions you set, buy a gym membership for, and then forget about. Intentions are renewed day by day, moment by moment. With intention, you set your compass toward what you want and then choose to walk in that direction in the only time you have: this moment.

With a new life entering your world, the opportunity to be intentional grows exponentially. Now, each moment with your little one is the opportunity to choose to be intentional with them, to make your moments together count, to be present during your shared moments, to make your words and actions meaningful, and to instill your values into their life. Whether you are painting their nursery, reading them a book, or changing their diaper, you can Nurture your child with intentionality.

Choose Your Direction

As much as we would love to tell you that you just "put it out there" and it comes to you, there is a little more to it. Being intentional requires dedication. You have to *set your compass* and then you have to *keep checking it*. You have to get clear on the things you want, that bring you joy, that fill you up, so you have more energy for what matters most, for what raises you, and what gets you where you want to be.

In order to live your values, you have to know your values. What direction do you want to head in? What direction do you want your child to head in?

Here are some questions you can ask yourself. If you want to write your answers out, you'll find a printable version in the companion workbook at NurtureMethod.com. You can also answer them in your mind, meditate on them, use them as discussion questions with a partner or loved one, or come back to them later.

- What are you most grateful for in your life?
- What do you want more of in your life?
- What are some traits about yourself that you would like to grow?
- Who are the people you admire most? What traits do they have that you admire?
- What are some cherished moments in your life? What was special about those moments?

- What do you think makes someone a "good" person?
- What do you wish for your child?
- What do you wish for your loved ones?
- What do you wish for the world?

Once you explore these questions, then you can look at them for common themes that help you get to your core values:

- What patterns or common threads do I see in my answers?
- What emotions or feelings are associated with my answers?
- What values or principles are implied in my answers?
- How do my answers reflect my relationships or connections with others?
- What do my answers say about my sense of purpose or meaning?

Whatever your answers, whatever your values, don't judge them or try change them into what you think they should be. What is important to you is what is important to you, and if you set your compass to someone else's true north, you will get lost very quickly.

Follow Your Path

Intentionality, like all of mindfulness, is not a full-time activity. If you are hiking and only staring at your compass, you're likely to break your ankle when you fall into the rabbit hole you missed or smack your head on a branch you didn't see. You have to take your eyes off the compass, watch where you are going, take in the views, stop for bathroom breaks, and *then* check your compass again. It is a constant give-and-take process.

The Nurture Method gives you some ways to bring intention into your daily life with your child, but it's important to bring intentionality into your own life, to check your own compass from time to time. If you make this practice part of your everyday life, you will find that it becomes easier to bring into your life as a caregiver. Below are some ways to check your own compass:

- *Every Morning.* Begin each day with the intention to live your values. You might say, "May I bring *kindness* to my words, thoughts,

and actions," or "May I use this day to become in tune with my values." For greater accountability you may want to say it aloud to yourself, to someone else, or write it down. If you feel overwhelmed by certain tasks, change language from "I have to do this" to "I get to do this." It changes the energy behind it and may help you stay in alignment with your values.
- *Every Night.* At the end of the day, reflect back. How did your thoughts, feelings, and actions align with the intention you set in the morning? If you didn't set an intention, then simply reflect on whether your actions and experiences aligned with your values. This is not an opportunity to keep score or judge yourself, but merely a practice to teach your mind to occasionally check your compass.
- *Every Day, here or there.* Pick one thing that you can do today that embodies your intention or puts your value into action. You could send a friend an affirming message, give your partner a hug before speaking, donate to a cause that is important to you, check in on a neighbor, cook a healthy meal. When you are able, do that thing—with intention. Be joyful at this chance to live your values in a meaningful way, and know that you are supporting yourself, your family, and the planet each time you act in alignment to your higher purpose.
- *Reflect on the above questions from time to time.* See if your values have changed, grown stronger, or if some have become more important than others.

Enjoy the Trip

Please don't forget that intentionality is not about perfection. Your path will ebb and flow, and your practices will ebb and flow. That's because life ebbs and flows.

Taking care of a child is hard. It's easy to fall back into old patterns, especially when your baby becomes a little older and life returns to more like how it was. But by continuing to set your intention and taking action, you can create lasting positive changes that are in alignment with what you want.

Intentionality is one of the best gifts you can give yourself and those around you. It moves you closer to your ideal vision for yourself, your child, your career—and how you can be your highest self through all of it. It helps you to create space for more of the good stuff that leads to your greater well-being. The more wholehearted you are, the greater joy, meaning, and love you have in your relationships and life, and this wholeheartedness will help you move through the natural challenges and hurdles that will come.

THE NURTURE METHOD AND YOU

As we'll explore in the next part, you can take these concepts of stillness, observation, and intention and fold them into whatever you do. But ultimately, they are yours to use however and whenever it serves you best. Trying to do it all and do it all perfectly is not the purpose of mindfulness and certainly not the purpose of the Nurture Method.

Remember to be kind and give yourself grace. Sometimes (many times!) you won't have the energy or desire to try and incorporate anything into your day other than to lean into the sheer will to get through it. Sometimes the most mindful thing you can do for yourself is *not* practice mindfulness. Mindfulness is about making the choices that are right for you, in the moment. It means coming back again and again. So do what you can, when you can. And when you can't, don't. Without judgement. And when you're ready, come back. The practice—stillness, observation, and intention—will be waiting, ready to support you on your journey with your child and beyond.

PART 2

TECHNIQUES

3

Words

OVERVIEW

The Nurture Method and Words

Stillness: Create some space between what happens around you and what you say. Allow your baby to take in the sounds you are making.
Observation: Notice how the words you think and say feel in your body and how your baby responds.
Intention: Take a moment to affirm your intention, the energy behind what you do or say, before speaking it into existence.

It is said that what we think about we bring about. Thoughts come and go, but each of us chooses the thoughts we focus on, which in turn become the words we speak that guide the actions we take. By being mindful of your words, you are modeling how to embrace life, grow through it (rather than just go through it), and maybe even find meaning and see the good in it.

HOW IT WORKS

Did you know that your mind doesn't just passively experience the world as it is, but instead actively creates your reality by the consciousness (or energy behind) the thoughts you think? The energy of your thoughts, your consciousness, impacts your level of well-being, moment by moment. Yes, *words can shape your reality.* The more you hear, think, and say negative words and phrases, the more likely you *and your little one* are to see your experiences and situations in that negative light. In other words, you have the power to manifest what you think most about. It might sound like something out of Harry Potter, but it's just science.

Here, let's prove it:
Stop and think about a lemon.
Really picture it.

The round, bright yellow fruit. Feel its weight in your hand. The tiny craters on its smooth skin. Now picture slicing it open. Your knife cutting through and little sprays of juice squirting out, dusting your skin. See the perfect round disc you cut, dimpled with a few seeds. And now imagine taking the slice of lemon and putting it in your mouth. Take a big bite and feel the mind-numbing sourness flood your mouth. Your eyes close and your lips pucker as the sensation overwhelms your tongue almost painfully but not quite.

Okay, back to real life.
Are you salivating right now?
Wild, right?

The reason is because your brain can't tell the difference between fantasy and reality. You *thought* you were eating a lemon so your brain told your body that you actually were.

Thoughts Lead to Things

The placebo effect is another example of how "thoughts lead to things" plays out in our lives. People can sometimes get better from a sickness or even a disease if they merely believe they are being treated for it, even if the treatment itself was actually nothing at all, a placebo. This works not only through the thoughts you think yourself, but also from what is told to you. When someone you trust, like your doctor, tells you this will make you feel better, it can, in some cases, lead to you actually feeling better. The placebo effect shows the power words have in shaping our reality.

So now imagine what happens if you say, "I'm a bad parent" over and over. Those words become the placebo your brain thinks is medicine, the juicy lemon that your brain takes a bite out of, and "I'm a bad parent" slowly becomes a self-fulfilling prophecy. Repeated thoughts or messages you say or you hear regularly eventually shape your narrative and become the filter through which you experience life.

Researchers at Stanford are among many people who are exploring exactly how the activity of your mind shapes your reality. Alia Crum, assistant professor of psychology and director of the Stanford Mind and Body Lab[1] said, "It's essential to recognize that mindsets are not peripheral, but central to health and behavior. If we truly want to tackle the diseases and crises of our time, we need to more effectively acknowledge and leverage the power of mindset."

Mindset Matters

Mindset is your set of beliefs, attitudes, and thoughts or in essence, the *words* that you think about moment to moment. We know outer circumstances are always changing. Nothing is permanent. Yet sometimes we hold on to beliefs that no longer serve us in our current circumstances. The question becomes: is your mindset based on what you are perceiving right now in this moment, or is it stuck on what happened twenty minutes ago, yesterday, or years ago? If your mind is fixated on something in your past or a possibility in the future, you may miss out on the good right here and now. Often this moment, right now, is just fine. But that is not where your mind is. You have the power to change your mindset. It's not easy. But it's possible.

The power of one's mindset was made evident in a study that looked at how people ease pain. The same researchers at Stanford found that "pain is highly responsive to each person's psychology and mindset." In a nutshell, the study showed that those who expect worse pain and feel helpless about it *suffer more* than those who have a more positive mindset and expectation for managing the pain.

So what are your choices? To have a fixed mindset (expecting the worst) or a growth mindset (being open to the good). A fixed mindset is easier in the short run but in the long run, putting in the effort to develop a growth mindset that is more in alignment with what you desire in your life and what you want to experience more of will bring you more joy.

Tara Swart, a neuroscientist, medical doctor, and lecturer at MIT Sloan, says in her book *The Source*[2] that, "When you do allow your brain to be conscious of and focus on what you want in life, the raised awareness that results will work in your favor to automatically bring opportunities into your life." In other words, science confirms that thoughts become things.

This is the work. In the choices you make day by day, moment by moment, you become more aware and begin to change the thoughts you have, the narrative you run, the words you say—all for the better. Parenting ignites a little spark to be better because the words we say shape our child's inner voice—so ask yourself, *what kind of things do we want that voice to say?*

TECHNIQUES

Notice and Allow

"Sticks and stones may break my bones, but names will never hurt me." You probably grew up with that phrase in your repertoire. Where along the line did we start teaching each other that words can't hurt us? We all know deep down it's not true.

Words, whether squiggles of soundwaves or lines on a screen, have immense power. Have you ever felt that sting of someone saying something to you that was hurtful? You might have been feeling good and *zap*, the words struck something inside you and it hurt. Someone can say something negative to you that immediately shifts your mood and energy. Conversely, someone can say something positive that lightens your mood and raises you up.

Words can boost you on to the finish line when you feel like you can't take another step forward. Or they can stop you in your tracks by reinforcing negative beliefs you already have. For instance, your partner can say something as simple as, "Why is the baby crying?" and it can set off a rollercoaster of thoughts. Perhaps you thought you'd had things under control, but that question made you think otherwise. Or perhaps you already had negative feelings inside you of not being good enough, unsure of what to do, and losing confidence, and then those five words were all you needed to confirm your falsely held belief and trigger feelings of shame, unworthiness, not being good enough.

So the very first step in creating a Nurturing practice around words is simply to notice them and acknowledge their power. Before you start changing your words, start noticing them. Notice how you use them, but almost more importantly, notice how you *perceive* them.

This might feel like a daunting task, and it is if you think you're going to observe the more than 10,000 words per day that we speak on average (not to mention the words everyone around you is speaking!). That's not only impossible but also not what the Nurture Method is about. This act of observing and acknowledging is a gentle practice that you can incorporate into your day without stress.

As you go about exploring words, your goal is simply to observe when something observable arises. For example:

1) If you have a response, positive or negative, to something someone said;
2) If you say something that gets a positive or negative response from someone;
3) If you see or hear a word that touches or triggers you in some way.

Noticing is not about judging. Notice the word by bringing gentle awareness to it. When you notice a word, don't decide that anything was good or bad. Simply identify it. "Wow, there it is. That word had power."

This act of that observation has a waterfall effect. With observation comes the ability to be intentional about how you speak and how you respond. And when you wield power over words, instead of the other way around, you have intention in the words you choose and responses you have, creating more space to be present and happy with your little one. Then, when they are old enough to begin using their own words, you will have the skills to help them observe and acknowledge the power of words, so that when the time comes that someone tells them, "Names will never hurt me," they will know there's much more to the story.

Shift Your Focus

There's an old saying that only a fool tries to outrun the raindrops. The message being that the rain will get you wet no matter what—so what do you want your experience to be? Do you want to accept that you're going to get wet, maybe even dance in the rain, or do you want to be frustrated trying to avoid something you can't? It's not a perfect proverb, but it does hit a truth about life: you can't outrun reality. So, what experience will you choose to have with what comes up?

As a parent, you help shape your child's experience by how you respond to the raindrops of life. And one of the ways they experience your response is from, yes, your words. This does not mean putting on rose-colored glasses and telling your child that everything is great when it's not. The Buddha said, "Life is suffering." Can't get any less rose-colored than that. Yet even amid suffering, you can discover acceptance, peace, and even joy by knowing and embracing the colorful, multifaceted nature of the human experience. Let's look at some of the ways to do that.

Talk about what's right

We're all guilty of talking more on what's going wrong instead of right or on an adopted belief or two (who's counting?) that you are not good enough or worthy of this or that. It's a little bit of both nature and nurture at work there. As humans, we tend to focus on the one negative thing. We are wired that way. It kept us safe from tigers lurking around the corner at one time in our existence. But we're also inundated with fear-inducing messages from media because frankly, "bad news sells." While that may be the reality in the outer world, your inner world and your home can be different. Our nature is not fear and insecurity. It's love. That's why the fear and insecure feelings make us feel so bad. It's not our nature. It just takes some work to make a different choice.

Now that you've begun to notice words and how they impact you, start to notice what words you use to describe what's happening around you. Do you tend to talk about the one negative thing? How does that shift the mood for you and then your baby?

Centering yourself in acceptance of *what is* instead of *what perfect is* or *what could have been* can be hard for many of us, but it is a powerful practice toward feeling better about your current situation. One easy, albeit silly, example is . . . poopy diapers! Do you say, "Ewwww, you've got a stinky diaper" to your cutie when you change them? Or worse when they have one of their explosions and it's not only seeping out of their diaper and onto that white outfit your aunt gifted you, but it's all over your shirt too.

Poopy diapers are *gross* and parenting is too sometimes. But is the gross factor the only thing to focus on? You could focus on how well they ate, how amazing their tiny little digestive system is, how nicely they're lying on the changing table, or how amazing that baby detergent is that it gets every brown, green, and yellow spot out of those white newborn clothes. As your baby ages and you are in potty training mode, you can quickly see how your own beliefs about potty-related things get picked up by your little one. So if you have that "icky poop" mentality, before long, so will they. You'll see how quickly what you focus on spreads to those around you.

Here are a few examples of other ways to talk about what's right!

- Instead of "Wow, you made a mess with the food!" try "You sure had a lot of fun trying new tastes and textures, didn't you?"
- Instead of "Rain is ruining our plans!" try "What a great excuse to stay inside and play together!"
- Instead of "I'm so tired, why won't you sleep?" try "I know we're both so tired and this is hard but I'm here for you and we'll get through this."
- Instead of "Why are you being so fussy?!" try "You're sure doing a great job telling me you need something, now let me figure out what it is."
- Instead of "You're not latching correctly!" try "We're figuring this out together, and it's okay if it takes a few tries."

Sprinkle in appreciation in this moment

The more you practice talking about what you appreciate in the moment, the more you'll find that you appreciate. It works the same as positive reinforcement: the more you reward positive behavior, as it is occurring, the more successful in making a behavior change. Just wait, you'll see this in action when you are working on changing behaviors when your little one is in their *terrible-twos* or *three-nager* stages. You may as well start practicing now.

Use these practices to help you make those positive choices.

- *Perspective Shift:* Think about something within your parenting where you'd like to make a change or you feel stuck, like responding in anger too easily, having little patience, or comparing yourself to a neighbor who seems to have it all figured out and leaves you feeling less-than. Now look at your experience from someone else's perspective. For example, someone without children who is struggling to conceive. Or an older person with only grown children living on their own. Or yourself ten years ago or ten years from now. Seeing your current situation from the perspective of someone else (or yourself in a different life stage) may change your perspective on it. A perspective shift helps you remember the journey and better appreciate where you are now.
- *Positive Visualization:* Use visualization to mentally walk through your day ahead or the experience that's causing you stress. Step through the experience as you'd like to show up, as your higher self. What actions would you take, how would you feel, what would unfold. Remember the lemon exercise from the start of this chapter? Our minds don't know the difference. If you see it in your mind, you can be it.
- *Questioning Your Story:* Ask different questions and change your story. When you say, "Why me?" or "Why does this always happen?" could be shifted to "What am I meant to learn from this?" or "How is this helping me grow?" Instead of "Why do bad things happen," it could be "What is the good in this?" With awareness and practice, you can ask different questions, and see your current situation differently.
- *Check Your Compass:* In chapter 2, we invited you to "choose your direction" by getting clarity on your values. If you didn't do that, now would be a great time to go back and complete that exercise (you'll find the questions in the companion workbook at NurtureMethod.com). Sometimes, reflecting on your values can change how you view your worries. You might realize they're not worth your energy and could use an affirmation to help reset your perspective.
- *Clear:* If worrying thoughts consume you, instead of allowing those negative thoughts to swirl and swallow you, pause and say "clear" or "cancel" to deny the negative or limited belief that's come over you. Next you can affirm a positive thought that will help you move

through the worry or challenge, maybe using a mantra. More on this coming up in chapter 5.

Let It Go

Sometimes you just have to let it go. Go ahead and belt it out just like Elsa in *Frozen*. She is onto something. Sometimes you say something without even recognizing the weight of it. Phrases such as, "this is the worst" or "I am dying" may just be expressions, but our brains can't always tell the difference between fantasy and reality as we saw with the lemon experiment. What reality are you creating when you define the world around you with such sweeping, critical, phrases? Here are some ways to shape that up and ship it out.

- *Make a list of some of your go-tos.* Make a list of your negative talk. Return to your list and maybe even say out loud, "That's a phrase I'd like to drop" (no surprise, stating aloud something you want to change is a proven way to make change).
- *Replace that list with some positive words and phrases.* What you have to say won't always be positive, but that's okay. As we said, your job isn't to use your words to create a world of unicorns and rainbows. Instead, use your words to let go of the judgment and create room for growth, understanding, support, empathy, and love. If your baby is driving you crazy, and they will, be intentional about what it is you are feeling and what you need. Unlike "He's driving me crazy," saying, "I haven't slept more than a few hours in days. I need help so I can take a nap," or, "I'm feeling so frustrated that I can't figure out what the baby wants" can make space for something constructive to happen.
- *Criticisms vs. compliments.* Take note of how often you are criticizing vs. complimenting. This can be powerful practice for the way you talk to yourself, your partner, and of course your child. You can make a tally list and begin keeping track of it to make the shift toward fewer criticisms and more compliments. You never know, posting that tally board in a highly visible spot in your home may even stir up some healthy competition. You can throw in some rewards, hello positive reinforcement, and you'll be positive self-talk, full steam ahead.

Choose Self-Compassion

When you can't seem to *let it go* . . . practice self-compassion. Compassion is a natural feeling that arises when you are confronted with suffering and you feel motivated to relieve that suffering. However, noticing your own suffering and trying to relieve it is not always as easy as doing it for someone else. It's too easy for parents to get into a place of judging, being critical, and even feeling inadequate—especially today in cruel Facebook groups and impossible to achieve Insta-photos.

Practicing self-compassion is a natural way to move beyond hurtful words that you are repeating to yourself and that make you feel anxious or even depressed. It can help you realize that you are not alone in feeling these things. Practicing self-compassion helps you recognize when you are suffering and allows you to be kind to yourself in that moment. With practice, you gain more awareness of this negative way of thinking and begin to respond differently, with compassion. Kristin Neff, PhD, widely recognized as one of the world's leading experts on self-compassion, shares how to be kind to yourself when you are suffering by practicing self-compassion in these three simple steps:[3]

1. *Recognize what you are feeling as you are feeling it:* Say to yourself: I feel sad. I feel mad. I feel disappointed. You may have learned to push these feelings down. As you do that, the feeling only grows and becomes harder to move through. Recognize what is coming up, accept it, and affirm that feeling a range of feelings is human.
2. *Zoom out:* Recognize that you are not alone in feeling this. You're not alone in having feelings like this and other people feel this way too. Sometimes it is in moments like this you isolate yourself and think you are the only one that struggles or that you don't deserve to be relieved of this suffering. This is not true.
3. *Love:* Extend kindness to yourself. Put your hands on your heart and extend love. Feel warmth and gentle touch. You could say: May I feel love, May I feel peace, I am enough, I am strong, I did the best I could, I forgive myself, I am enough.

Self-compassion is a powerful way to use your words. The practice of self-compassion can help you when you are in a place of suffering so you can move through it lovingly. When you practice self-compassion in front of your child, you give them a skill that they can begin to use on themselves and others, and this is invaluable.

Choose Love

It's not always the easy choice, but it's the right choice. You'll never regret the choice to take a moment to pause and choose love, making that the energy behind what you do and say in your home. It's worth the work because the way you treat people matters, and it starts with how you treat yourself. And is there any better lesson to model to our children than *the way you treat people matters?* In the words of Maya Angelou, "People will forget what you said, they will forget what you did, but they will never forget how you made them feel."

Remember, Little by Little

Little steps. Small shifts. You won't change the way you say things overnight. Pick one thing in your day that you want to approach differently, that is within your power to shift what you think and say about it. You can't change the unexpected occurrence of diaper explosions. They just happen, but maybe it does start at the changing table. In this one location, every time you grab a new diaper, you will choose to focus on something good. I am grateful for . . . and say it aloud.

Or it could be during playtime. Instead of saying, "Wow, what a mess!" You could say, "We had a lot of fun. Time to clean up!" It could be when you're exhausted and haven't showered in days and this is nothing like you imagined life with your baby would be and you just want to say, "I don't know if I'm cut out for this." Can you instead say, "I'm proud of myself for pressing on even when I'm feeling this way?" What you focus on matters and energy flows where your attention goes. Be responsible for the words you say and begin noticing the energy they have and how it positively (or negatively at times) is felt by those around you. Small consistent improvements lead to big change.

4

Songs

OVERVIEW

The Nurture Method and Songs

Stillness: Listen to a song without distraction or agenda, allowing the music to be present and evoke any emotions, thoughts, or physical sensations.

Observation: Notice the various sounds, instruments, textures, and messages within the music, paying attention to how it makes you and your little one feel physically and emotionally.

Intention: Reflect on how you can intentionally use sound and song to center your being, elevate your experience with your child, and connect with your emotions and inner self.

Babies respond to music and song—even in the womb. We all come into the world with an innate capacity for responding to and making music. New studies show that babies likely start hearing sounds in the second trimester and really begin to respond to noises during the final trimester. It's no surprise then that music is such a big part of children's lives, which is why it is one of the best go-tos for sprinkling some Nurturing into your day!

How It Works

Songs have a more profound impact than words alone. Songs are felt through their rhythm and melody, as well as their words. They stay with you thanks to their consistent patterns and structure. But more than that, songs make you smile, cry, laugh, reminisce. They make you feel comforted, loved, understood. Songs go beyond your mind and connect right to your heart and soul.

Why is it that music has such a distinct impact on us? Scientists have long thought there is some sort of musical center in the brain but haven't been able to prove it. Recently, though, researchers at MIT discovered a dedicated neural pathway that's all about music. What's really cool is that this pathway is separate from the ones that process other sounds, and is actually on the *same level as the one for speech*. This means that our brains are wired to treat music as a fundamental part of our lives![1] It's no wonder, then, that babies who haven't yet learned to speak respond so much to music!

Studies[2] have shown that music has numerous benefits for babies, including:

- Improved cognitive development
- Enhanced language skills
- Better memory and spatial-temporal skills
- Reduced stress and anxiety
- Improved mood and emotional regulation

Music is so amazing that research has shown that premature babies who listen to soft music or humming gain weight faster and leave intensive care units earlier! Music is a powerful tool for infants, and it can be a valuable way to connect with your baby.[3]

Knowing that music can almost, quite literally, speak to your baby, you can begin to understand why song and music is one of the best ways to connect with your little one. Think about this: babies under the age of one don't even understand the concept of yes and no. The logic centers of their brain aren't formed yet, so if you are trying to understand your child from a place of logic, you'll have trouble connecting and empathizing with them. That's where the magic of song comes in. Children tune into it naturally; they feel it as if you are speaking to them. Even as children get older and begin to understand and start communicating, you can teach and connect with them through song. It has a different energy than words alone. It doesn't matter which type of music you share as much as choosing music that sounds and feels good to you.

The elements of the Nurture Method come together when you listen to music or create your own. You can move or listen quietly, but when you approach music with intention, stillness, and observation, your body, mind, and soul respond to the vibrations, and an energy shift occurs, unifying all parts of you.

As you listen to music with your baby, practice being present. Observe how you and your baby respond to different types of music and stillness. Notice how it affects your mood and temperament. Invite curiosity and explore different styles to see what works best for you and your baby. With so many ways to access music today, you can easily incorporate it into your daily routine. Use it as a tool to set the tone, recenter, and nurture your connection with your baby. See how songs can make you feel from the inside out, and watch your baby thrive in response to the power of music.

TECHNIQUES

Feed Your Soul

Music can be comforting like your most cherished meal from home, succulent like a five-course dinner at your favorite restaurant, healing like a freshly made salad, or sheer delight like your guilty-pleasure candy. And just like food, it often takes effort to not go straight for the candy—the catchiest, poppiest, foot-tappingest, top of the charts stuff, not only because it's the most fun, but also because it's easy for companies to sell us on it. Quick and inexpensive to produce, a bag of M&Ms makes for a much better commercial than an organic head of lettuce. The same goes for music which is easy to produce, easy to market, and easy to sell when it's sugary sweet and loaded with words, music, and performances that are designed for instant pleasure. There's nothing wrong with that, just like there's nothing wrong with a bag of M&Ms, but our bodies need so much more when it comes to food and music. Children's music today is especially made to be sugary sweet, loaded with wacky voices, silly sound effects, and a cacophony of instruments, all designed to distract rather than support.

Your little one will use the songs you play for them as a learning tool, it will help them connect to you as you sing and dance with them, it will teach them language, teach them music, teach them about the world, and as we looked at above, it will even produce changes in the brain. So as a Nurturing practice, begin to bring intention into what music you feed to them.

Discover the Stories

Have you ever sung along to a song and realized that you're only just then understanding what the song is about? Sometimes, we fall in love with a song's beat or feel without ever putting it all together and understanding what the song is actually about. But each song has a unique story that it tells through its lyrics, melody, instruments, and the mood it evokes. When you can, take time to observe how these components come together to create an entire story, and pay attention to what that story sparks in you. Is that story something you would read to your little one in a book? Is it evoking feelings that you want to share with your child?

Explore the Beat

Songs don't have to have words. As you listen to music, pay attention to *the music.* What does the beat do to you? Do some songs make your heart beat a little faster or others make you feel like you're wrapped up in a warm blanket? Do some bouncy tunes make you smile for reasons you can't even explain or other soft melodies fill you with a sense of yearning? If you experience sensations from listening to songs, imagine what your child is feeling, even if they can't show you. If you find the music loud and annoying, maybe that's a clue. Even if your child enjoys it, remember that they will also eat sweets for breakfast, lunch, and dinner, so just because they like it doesn't mean it's the only thing you give them. You can offer certain music as a treat rather than as the main course of music.

Enter the Silence

Stick with us on this one. Pauses and breaks are *part* of a song. They're written in, just in the same way the notes are. Silence allows us time to appreciate, to imagine, to enjoy, to anticipate. Even the tiniest little ones can take pleasure in, or play in the silence. Don't rush to fill the silence with a new song. Instead, give both of you an opportunity to connect in the quiet. You can even turn silence into a game by singing a song and leaving out a line. Your baby may actually try to fill in the missing words with a to-die-for babble, or they may watch you with rapt attention as they try to figure out what's missing. As they get old enough to see you clearly, you can really start to have fun with this. Try singing a verse of "The itsy-bitsy spider" out loud, then tell them you're going to sing about the very-quiet spider. As you move your mouth without singing, your wiggle monster will sit completely still as they listen for the very quiet spider.

Go Beyond Kids' Music

There is absolutely no rule that says you have to play kids songs for kids. The more music children are exposed to the better! Bring on the musical buffet—jazz, classical, country, pop, whatever is on your Spotify playlist, and try something new, too. And the more you are moving with the music, the better—clapping, stomping, patting, dancing, and singing creates more meaning. Plus, if you are enjoying and engaging in the music, then your baby will benefit from the energy you bring. Remember to bring your observation to these songs to try to make sure the beats and stories are nourishing for you both.

You'll find some suggestions for music to get you started in the companion workbook at NurtureMethod.com.

Make Your Own Music

Here's the best-kept secret: according to your baby, *you* are the best singer out there. Creating your own music is not only fun, but it can also help with daily activities and routines. Complaints about loading into the car seat become giggles when you make it into a musical event. And just the way you will never forget how to sing Old MacDonald, the songs you create with your little one will stay with them and Nurture them as they grow older. It can help them remember steps in an activity or concepts about the world, but most importantly, it will remind them of love and comfort and their connection with you. Not sure how to create your own, loving, mindful music? Here's some easy ways to get started:

Play with words and sounds

You don't need a special class to bring Nurturing music into your baby's world. You might feel a little awkward, a little silly, a little unsure, but there's only one way to get over that and that's to get started! We assure you that even if you feel you can't carry a tune, your child won't even notice. *They love to hear your voice in this way.*

Use that creative essence and your exploration into music to just *dive in*. Bring your own words, beats, and tunes to delight and calm your baby. Here are some ideas to help you on your way:

Rhyme

You know how that goes! Dr. Seuss reminds us that we don't even need actual words to make a rhyme. Made-up words and silly sounds work perfectly well! Lovey Dovey. A rat tat tat. A rat tat tat. Oh My Sweetie Pie, I love you, Yes I do.

Simile and metaphor

Compare things around you. Your cheeks are as smooth as silk. Your little toes are sweeter than pie. This tool is also helpful when we are teaching children, because comparing is a fun way to remember things.

Repetition

Repeat, repeat, repeat. Babies learn by repetition, so the more you say it, the easier it is for them to pick up when they begin "using their words."

Alliteration

This is fun to bring in as you put together strings of words that start with the same sound. It helps in the early literacy process by building memory skills and phonics awareness. As you are eating with your baby, you can enjoy foods such as "super sweet strawberries" or "tart and tangy tangerines" or let them know "creamy cauliflower coming closer." Get ready for the giggles as it becomes a tongue twister and you say something like, "Peter Piper picked a peck of pickled peppers. If Peter Piper picked a peck of pickled peppers, where's the peck of pickled peppers Peter Piper picked?"

Personification

Children love this. It's all about giving human traits to something that is not human, like Mr. Toothbrush. You don't want to leave Ms. Carrot all by herself there on your plate? Why don't you eat it up so it can be with all the other carrots inside your tummy?

Pick a theme

Ask questions, teach, encourage, and turn everyday conversations into music with your little one's rhythm. Here's a few to try out.
How do you feel?
You can model for your child by singing songs about how you feel—happy, sad, angry, silly, or whatever. Learning at an early age to focus on how they feel is a really great practice for when they get into toddlerhood and start being aware of and communicating about their feelings. It goes back to children being all energy and emotion. As we model expressing how we are feeling for them—and we can do that in songs—we are modeling how they can work through their own emotions too.
You are special!
Kick it back into Mr. Rogers style. He was the king of very simple songs that kids just connect to. Simple songs like, "Today is special, you are special by being you, just the way you are. No one quite like you. Just be you. I like you just as you are." You can say it any way you like that feels good for you. Words repeated often become their inner monologue, so make them matter, since your little one matters most to you. We love how Dr. Seuss brilliantly put it: "Be who you are and say what you feel because those who mind don't matter and those who matter don't mind."

Head, shoulders, knees, and toes

Ready to teach your little one about their body parts plus get some movement and stretching in? It doesn't get much better than *"head, shoulders, knees and toes knees and toes!"* This one is a great one for starting the day, ending the day, or in the middle for transitions or just getting their wiggles out.

Just do your best, your best is the best for you!

This one comes from a preschool favorite, Daniel Tiger. If you're looking for a catchy song to teach a needed lesson to your preschooler, look no further than Daniel Tiger. One that you can use a lot, especially when your little one is struggling, frustrated, or losing his patience with something new is *"just do your best, your best is the best for you."* Your little one will melt into you instead of melt down.

Using common melodies to create new songs

There are certain songs that are just easy to free flow with. Anyone can break into a hum of one of these songs without a hitch. This is a great way to start making up your own songs; just take a melody you know, put your own words to it, and sing about anything that you are doing, feeling, or thinking about.

For instance, you might change the words to "London Bridge Is Falling Down" *to:*

Change Your Diaper,
Here we go, Here we go, Here we go,
Change Your Diaper
Here we go
My Sweet Baby

Or change "You Are My Sunshine" *to a bedtime song like:*

You are my sweet one, my tired sweet one
It's time to close eyes and go to bed
You know I love you, my tired sweet one
Now let's close eyes and go to bed

Rewrite "Here We Go Round the Mulberry Bush" *for any activity that's part of your routine. For example:*

This is the way we make a bottle
Make a bottle
Make a bottle
This is the way we make a bottle
Early in the morning

You get the idea, just go with whatever comes to mind. Let it flow.

Good night bedtime song

This may be what you think of first when you think of songs. Lullabies are such a wonderful way to help your baby fall asleep. It's helpful to have a few to sing. There may be some you make up yourself, like we mentioned above, that may become part of your bedtime ritual. Or sing a traditional lullaby that you remember from when you were young. Babies love the sound of your voice and the rhythm of a song more than anything. Here are a few more ideas:

Make up your own Good Night Song. Something like:

Good Night
Sleep Tight
I'll see you in the morning
Good night
Sleep tight
Tomorrow's a new day.

Try one of these classics.

- *Baby Beluga*
- *You Are My Sunshine*
- *Lavender's Blue Dilly Dilly*
- *Rock a Bye Baby*
- *If You're Happy and You Know It*
- *Row, Row, Row Your Boat*
- *Twinkle, Twinkle, Little Star*

Tap into your creativity

Creating music not only helps your baby, but it helps you too. When you connect with music, you are in connection with your essential nature, where creativity, imagination, and love live. If you feel like you are not creative, or not creative enough, don't let your inner voice tell you what you are and are not. The fact is, every one of us is incredibly creative. Watching children will confirm that in a heartbeat. *Every* child is brimming with creativity. A child has no problem drawing a picture, singing a song, creating a game, or imagining a character.

Creativity is innate within all of us. Our bodies may have changed into an adult form, but much like children forget how to fly to Never-Never Land, it isn't that you can't do it, it's simply that you've forgotten how. Too often adults lose their creative spark due to the influence of others telling them they are not good enough (because as we discuss in chapter 3, words are powerful!). Your creative spark is there and ready to be ignited again. That's one of the great joys of having children, they are our very own Peter Pans, bringing fairy dust and the directions back to Never-Never Land (it's the third star on the right, then straight on 'til morning, in case you needed a reminder).

Here are some ways to let your guard down and creativity in. You can:

- Watch their goofy faces, their silly noises, their intense fascination with how their body moves and then see what comes up for you.
- Match their faces or noises or create your own range of facial expressions with sounds that match the mood: excited, angry, surprised . . . you get the idea.
- Talk to them, whatever you want to say, just let it out.
- Rediscover what your own body can do and find it just as fascinating as your child does as you wiggle and giggle as the spirit moves you.

And all of that—it's creativity. It's plugging into the part of you that can express yourself and your world. Babies don't judge, they just love you as you are, and the more "you" you let out, the more they love you. This is how they learn it's okay to let their whole self show too.

5

Mantra

OVERVIEW

The Nurture Method and Mantra

Stillness: Allow the mantra to help your mind and body relax and become still.

Observation: Notice the sound, sensation, and meaning of the mantra as you repeat it, observing its effects on your mind and body and your baby's.

Intention: Choose and repeat a mantra that resonates with what you and your little one need. Say it, sharing the meaning with yourself and your baby.

The practice of repeating a mantra is a powerful tool for calming the mind, promoting positive thinking, and quieting the constant chatter of thoughts. By repeating a simple word or phrase, you become present and create a comforting vibration that can be shared with their baby. This ancient practice, used for centuries across most cultures, has been validated by modern science, and can be used by anyone to cultivate a more peaceful state of being for you and baby.

Chapter 5

HOW IT WORKS

The practice of repeating a mantra is a time-honored system that has been used throughout the world to help calm and relax your nervous system and promote positive thinking. It involves saying a word or short phrase repeatedly. Just like the Little Engine That Could repeated "I think I can" over and over again until she could; that's the basic premise of mantra. The words are not magical and the practice is not tied to any belief system. So while some ascribe a mystical quality to mantras, the reality is mantras are not religious. They are not tied to any faith or belief system. They're simply an age-old practice that packs a powerful punch. As always, if the spiritual side of mantras appeals to you, add that into your mantra practice. That's your own special flavor of mantras. The basic recipes we offer here serve three excellent, very down-to-earth purposes for us adults.

1. Quiet the Monkey Mind

Before there was Freud, there were yogis. These ancient scholars of the mind knew that there was more to our brain than just our thoughts. They knew that there was a true self that was separate from our thoughts and that could even *watch* our thoughts. Like many things in the yogic philosophy, modern science has come to agree: we are not our thoughts.

Our thoughts can't stop. In fact, they shouldn't stop. Our thoughts are just doing their job, like our heart is pumping blood and our lungs are taking in oxygen. If any of those things stop, it's not good.

But just because we're thinking doesn't mean that we, our true selves, have to engage with every thought that comes by. Easier said than done, of course. That's why our thoughts are often referred to as a "monkey mind." It's a great description because it's pretty easy to picture this little monkey in your brain leaping around, screeching loudly, swinging from thought to thought, and throwing a pile of . . . well, you know, your way.

That's where mantras come in.

Thankfully, yogis figured it out before *Psychology Today* was a twinkle in some editor's eye. If you give your monkey mind something to do, it gives your true self room to breathe. Your monkey is a simple little fellow, so you have to give him something easy to do. So that's why most mantras are short and sweet. Just one or two words repeated over and over and over and over in your mind, in your monkey mind, giving you, the true you, the space to—*ahhhhhhh*—just be present and be quiet.

Babies don't really have monkey minds yet. How lucky! But they will benefit from the benefits you receive. And when their own monkey minds develop, they will already have a practice to support them!

2. Manifestation

That's another one of those "out there" words that can have a metaphysical meaning. But *to manifest* is a verb that literally just means, "to clearly reveal to the mind or the senses or judgment." Mantras can help us clearly reveal the person we want to be, not by magic but by science. We've covered how words can shape our reality (read through the lemon exercise in the "How It Works" section of chapter 3 if you need a refresher!). The thoughts we think and the words we use tell our brains what we want and how we want to live.

If you're familiar with any mantras then you might be thinking, "aren't a lot of mantras in another language, like Sanskrit? How can I tell my brain something if it's in a language I don't speak?"

Yes, a lot of mantras are in another (often ancient) language. And that's okay. *In fact, we recommend using mantras that are in a language other than your native tongue.*

Here's why that's not a problem, and why we actually recommend it.

You don't need the word tree written on every tree to know it's a tree, right? You don't look at a tree and have to think to yourself, "That is a *tree*." You look at it and you just know it's a tree. It works the same way for mantras. Once you know the meaning, you just *know it*. You might be making sounds that aren't familiar words to you, but your brain has got the concept, it's got the intention, it's got the message. We recommend mantras that aren't in your native language for that very reason. When it comes to keeping your monkey mind busy, it can be really helpful to use something that comes without any baggage.

As an example, if you say, "I am peace" as your mantra, your monkey mind may make quick work of that. After a few repetitions you notice how weird the word peace is. And start to wonder why is it that there are two words, peace and piece, spelled completely differently and meaning totally different things but pronounced the exact same way. And what exactly does it mean to BE peace anyway? Is it a state of mind? Being? Doing? How does one DO peace? What does a piece of peace look like?

Or you could say, "Om shanti om." A simple wish for peace. Now as you repeat the words, you know the meaning but your mind can focus on just the sounds. You can relax into the sounds of *om shanti om* and into the knowledge that you are inviting peace into your life without getting caught up in what you associate with the words you're saying.

This is another one of those awesome two-for-one benefits. If you can manifest a happier, healthier, more peaceful brain, then you will see that manifesting in how you act around your baby. You will have more patience, more kindness, more gentleness, more grounding, and all around more positive mental space to give to your little one!

3. Vibration

This one is about as practical as it gets. Babies absolutely and completely *love* to feel vibrations. You know this all too well—put them in a car or a stroller and it's almost like a knock-out drug. But many babies especially love the sensation of our rumbly vocal cords too! It doesn't take a scientist to know why. They spent nine months *feeling* mom's voice. The comfort from this kind of vibration doesn't go away as we get older. Are you one of those people who fall asleep the moment a plane takes off? For many of us, the gentle hum of an engine or the consistent buzz of white noise is as strong as a big dose of Nyquil. One reason is that the sensation feels like home, like warmth and safety, and are you getting sleepy too just thinking about it?

We can recreate that comforting feeling in our own bodies when we repeat a mantra. Saying the same words over and over creates a comforting rhythm inside of ourselves. When we repeat a mantra with our babies, we share that soothing sensation with them. When you hold them, your chest rumbles gently and ushers them back to that safe and welcoming place. Even if they're not touching you, they still get the benefit of those vibrations (what else are words but vibration of sound waves?). That nice vibrating rhythm coming from their loved one is such a comforting treat.

TECHNIQUE

Mantra for All Seasons

As you explore *how* to use mantra, it's helpful to think about *when* you can use mantra. The answer is: pretty much always!

Here are a few ways you can incorporate mantra into your day:
If you've got a sleepy or snuggly baby, make this quiet time a meditative experience. Lay back, close your eyes, hold them close to your chest, and say your mantras out loud slowly and deeply. Let them enjoy the vibrations from your chest as you take a deep breath in and almost sing your mantra, holding each word for the length of a breath.

If you've got a wiggly baby, make your mantra a playful activity! Clap your hands to the mantra or better yet, clap their hands! Bicycle their legs to the rhythm. Or just wiggle with them as you repeat the words. Have fun and get creative!

If you've got a crabby baby, mantras are a great tool for your toolbox! You can sit with them and speak softly, letting your mantra be a gentle "shushing" sound. Or match their energy by putting them in their favorite hold and rocking or bouncing them to the sound of the mantra.

Use mantra as part of your *rituals* (chapter 10) for things like getting ready for sleep, starting the day, or heading out the door. Sing a mantra to make *diaper changes* a little bit more fun and playful. Instead of picking up your phone when it's time for yet another *feeding*, pick up a mantra. Reach for a mantra when *you* need *support* to get through a tough moment.

The possibilities for how and when to use mantra are nearly endless. You can only find what works for you and your baby by experimenting with this tool, but you will know when you find something that feels good for both of you.

1. Choose Your Mantra

Picking a mantra is like picking an ice cream flavor. Pick whichever one seems the most delicious! What do you need in the moment? What do you want more of in your day? What do you want for your child?

Mantras are available to you for a moment or a lifetime. You can select an ancient mantra, tried and true words that have been practiced for millennia, or you can make up your own by selecting a word or phrase that is meaningful to you.

A quick Google search will reveal an ocean of mantras to choose from. You can even Google "mantras for . . ." and fill in what you're in need of (Yes! Even, "help my baby sleep") to get more specific suggestions. Some mantra sites will lean into the mystical side of the practice or get downright car salesy, promising that all your wishes will be fulfilled if you chant this mantra enough. You can choose to explore that when you are looking for a mantra. Or not. Remember, this is your practice and you can build it in whatever way is supportive to you.

To begin your mantra practice, we've shared some of our absolute favorite mantras:

- *Om (or Aum)* (ah-oh-m): This is not a word from any language but is considered to be the sound of the universe. This calming mantra is an invitation to become connected with the world around you. Some research suggests that Aum may match the frequency of the universe—423 Hertz. As you chant Aum, picture yourself relaxing into the ocean in a tropical location so beautiful and warm you're not sure where you, the water, and the air begin or end.
- *Sat nam* (saht-nahm): A Gurmuhki word that means *truth is my identity*. This is a beautiful mantra for parents who can so quickly lose their identities in the hustle and bustle of a new baby. Between sleepless nights, undecipherable crying, and unsolicited advice, sometimes it can feel like we aren't sure who we are or if we're doing anything right. But in fact, we are. We can trust in our intuition and our love. The truth is available to you because it is your identity.
- *Pacem* (pach-em): A Latin word meaning "Peace." Is there anything else that parents are more in need of than a little peace? As you speak these words, feel them throughout your body, invite your mind to focus on the syllables and find peace in their simplicity.
- *Maum* (mah-oo-m): The Korean mantra meaning *mind*. Perhaps the perfect word for a *mind*fulness practice, wouldn't you say? Maum invites us to bring our minds back from the past, the future, the grocery lists, the errands, the housework, from all the things clogging up our mind and keeping us from being right here, right now.
- *Hamsa* (ha-m-sah): A Sanskrit word meaning *I am*. This is a grounding mantra that brings us back into our bodies, back into the

present moment. It is a calming mantra for your little one, as you can assure them, *I am* here, *I am* with you, *I am* supporting you.
- *Ho'oponopono* (ho-oh-poh-no-poh-no): A beautiful Hawaiian mantra that can be translated to mean, *I love you, I'm sorry, forgive me, thank you.* From the moment they arrive, our children show us our limitations. This mantra of reconciliation is a gift we need to offer ourselves and our babies on a regular basis, as a reminder that we are not perfect, but that is okay. We love ourselves, and our babies love us too.

Make your own

The best part about mantra is that you can make your own! Think of something positive that you want to share with yourself and your baby. Some possibilities might be:

- I am loving kindness
- Peace
- We are safe
- I am grateful
- I give love
- Peace begins with me
- I choose love

You can say those words as your mantra or, as we discussed earlier, it can be helpful to translate the words into another language to help you focus on the intention rather than the words. It doesn't have to be an exact translation; you might just choose the word "safe" to capture the meaning of your mantra. Your brain knows what you're going for and will absorb the meaning just fine.

2. Use Your Mantra

There's no magic to mantra. Here's all you need to do:

a. *Repeat the mantra in a rhythmic pattern.*

You can speak your mantra. It can be a quick beat like a drum: *sat nam, sat nam, sat nam, sat nam.* Or it can be drawn out like a sigh with a *saaaat* on the inhale and *naaaam* on the exhale. It could be something in between.

You can sing your mantra. In fact, the rhythm makes them naturally kind of musical. We're big fans of singing mantras. They make for really simple and fun songs that your baby will enjoy. You can come up with your own tunes (tips on that in chapter 4) or listen to mantra music. We've listed some of our favorite mantra albums on NurtureMethod.com.

You can say your mantra silently. Repeating mantras silently is commonly used for meditation practice, because it serves to hone your thoughts and settle your mind. Sure, verbalizing your mantra has the added benefit of sharing the sounds with your baby. However, if you say the mantras internally, they will support you, which in turn will support your baby.

b. *Try to say your mantra at least twenty to thirty times.*

And keep going even longer if you want to. You can also do it for 20–30 minutes. Or even longer! The more you do it, the more you and your baby get all the benefits, all the connection, all the support, all the joy that comes with mantra.

c. *Let it nourish you.*

As you repeat your mantra, stay present, stay with the mantra. Do your best not to get caught up in the meaning of the mantra or what it would look like in your life. Instead, focus on the *intention*. Let the words continually bring you back to the very moment you are in. Let the sounds quiet all the other thoughts of the past or the future, the laundry list of errands, the upcoming pediatrician appointment, the upcoming visit from family, the stain on the carpet, the backlog of e-mails. Let each repetition bring you back to what really matters, you and your little one. Envision the mantra as a magnet pulling in whatever it is you're repeating. See the sounds spilling out of you like a waterfall and enveloping your baby. Wrapped in the mantra, those magnetic words bring your wishes for peace, happiness, grounding, love, or whatever you desire to your baby.

If you ascribe to a particular faith, you are welcome to turn your mantra into a prayer. Mantras can be a really beautiful way to connect with your higher power and ask for what you want in your life.

6

Breath

OVERVIEW

The Nurture Method and Breath

Stillness: Allow your breath to calm and settle your mind and body, creating a peaceful atmosphere for you and your baby.
Observation: Notice the sensation of your breath, observing how it moves in and out of your body, and how it affects your mind, body, and your connection with your baby.
Intention: Focus on the breath, using it as a way to cultivate presence, calm, and connection.

By incorporating mindful breathing into your daily routine, you will be able to cultivate presence and clarity, allowing you to better respond to your baby's needs and emotions. With each breath, you'll nurture both your own well-being and your baby's, deepening your bond and connection.

HOW IT WORKS

Breathing is life.
But as adults, we've forgotten how to do it.
Sometimes we even forget *to* do it.

Next time you have a chance, watch your baby sleep. Once you get over how cute they look, take a peek at their breathing. Notice how their belly rises and falls with each breath. This is the untouched snow of breathing, not yet marred by the physical and emotional tolls that teaches our body to take shallow breaths. This belly (or diaphragmatic) breathing occurs when we use all our muscles the way we were intended and get a big, full breath of fresh air.

Over time, we forget how to do it. Instead, we take shallow breaths that never fully engage the diaphragm. Go check yourself out in a mirror and see if your breathing looks like your baby's. Probably not so much, right? We adults tend to breath up higher—instead of our bellies expanding, our chest and shoulders rise. There's a lot of reasons for that, and none of them are particularly great. We spend our days stressed, hunched over our phones and computers and bombarded with noise and pollution, wrangling the stress and anxiety of work and relationships and, oh yes, adorable but needy babies. And as a result, we almost never get the deep breaths our body needs.

The Problem with Shallow Breathing

Taking short, shallow breaths is supposed to be reserved for emergencies only. It's used when the "fight or flight" system is activated to get us oxygen quickly so our body has what it needs to either go into battle or run like the wind. But in the twenty-first century, the nonstop stimulation of life keeps our body in a state of perpetual fight or flight, which means we're almost always taking shallow breaths. But, as you can imagine, when we continually take shallow breaths that doesn't pan out well in the long run. Shallow breathing has been linked to all sorts of problems, like increased anxiety, higher blood pressure, lower immune system function, and back pain. And guess what, when you're anxious, sick, and in pain—*you take shallow breaths!*

In other words, the more you do it, the worse you feel, which causes you to do it more.

Returning to the Breath

Taking deep breaths is like medicine for the body. While shallow breathing is for the body's "fight or flight" mode, deep breathing is for our "rest and digest" mode. Literally, it activates the parasympathetic nervous system that tells our body that we're in a safe place and can relax and heal. Deep breathing:

- Fills our blood with life giving oxygen,
- Lowers our heart rate,
- Stabilizes or lowers our blood pressure, and
- Reduces stress.

And just like shallow breathing, it's a self-fulfilling prophecy. The more you let your body hang out in that state of "rest and digest," the better, more relaxed, more clear-headed you'll feel and the more you'll be able to take those wonderful belly breaths.

Sounds like heaven, right? Well, as Jesus taught, "You must become a child to enter the kingdom of heaven," and in this case, that's exactly what we need to do. If you want the heaven that comes with deep, oxygenated breaths, then you need to breathe like a child again.

Luckily we have our little ones to guide and inspire us.

How this Benefits Baby

Breathing support

When baby horses are born, they're on their feet within half an hour and can gallop by the end of the day.

Human babies? Not so much. After forty weeks or so of cooking, they've outgrown their oven, but they're not quite done baking. They come out still needing a lot of the things they were getting in the womb, and that includes the heartbeat and breathing that they were so connected to in the womb. That's why, as they continue to grow, our breathing helps their breathing. During the early months of infancy, gaps in breathing are very common, and it is believed that our breaths remind them to take that next inhale. Sometimes babies will even synchronize their breath to ours! How much more important is it, then, that we not only take long and healthy breaths but that we *share* them with our baby.

Healthy you

Is deep breathing going to cure all of life's ills and make you the best caregiver to your child? Unfortunately, no. We will still be stressed and frustrated, and we won't have the patience of a saint. But as we showed, deep breathing can help you feel better mentally and physically. And if you are just a little happier and healthier, how can that *not* benefit your little one?

TECHNIQUES

Breath is, perhaps, the most fundamental mindfulness technique available. Why? Because we're always breathing! Our inhales and exhales are there for us anytime. When you move from unconscious to intentional breathing, you move into the present moment. Your mind is able to grow still as it focuses on the simple action of air going in and out of your lungs.

The techniques we share here can be utilized on your own, to help you feel Nurtured so you can bring what you need to your baby, or you can share the benefits directly with them through the power of touch. Here are a few ways to do that:

- *Skin to skin* (also known as kangaroo care)—Strip your baby down to a diaper and place them directly on your bare chest.
- *Chest rest*—Kangaroo care with clothes on! Hold baby chest to chest.
- *Side lying*—Lie on your side and bring your baby in facing you (note: if you think you might fall asleep make sure you have a safe sleeping area).
- *In a baby carrier*—Strapping them to your chest is about as close together as you two can get!

As you begin to explore breathwork, you'll see how it supports you and you will find ways to incorporate it into your day. But to get you started thinking about when and where you can use these breathing techniques, here are a few suggestions:

- Going to sleep/having trouble sleeping: When you are up with your baby at 2:00 in the morning, begging them to go back to sleep, hold them close and use your breath. When they finally fall asleep and now you can't sleep, let your breath help you drift off.
- Breastfeeding/bottle feeding: Rather than grabbing your phone or turning on the TV when it's time for yet another feed, use this precious time to focus on and grow quiet with your breath.

- On a walk: When you go for an Adventure (chapter 9), strap your little one onto a carrier and share beautiful breaths together.
- During playtime: Incorporate breath into your activities and make it fun! When you exhale, blow out your air on your baby's body and watch the giggles. Bumblebee breathing is a great one, too, since it gets you making silly sounds that are sure to delight.
- During a meltdown: And we're not just talking about baby meltdowns. Yes, breathwork can help calm a screaming baby. But it can also help calm you when you're having a totally normal and totally understandable meltdown.
- When you're too exhausted to keep going: With a child, you will reach that point more times than you can count. Mindful breathing can help you stay present and intentional by giving your mind and body the Nurturing it needs to keep going just a little bit longer.

The techniques we share here are only a few of many types of breathwork, and we encourage you to explore further if you are interested. From yoga class, meditation class, online courses, even breathwork teachers, there are an almost endless number of ways to turn something as mundane as breathing into a powerful and healing experience. In the end, it's not about using a specific type of breathwork. You can accomplish all this without using any technique. Ultimately, this practice is about using your breath to become still, present, and intentional, and only you will know the best way to do that.

Note: Some breathing exercises you might learn or already use are "energizing" techniques designed to get your blood pumping and your heart thumping. While there are no contraindications for doing any kind of breathing techniques with babies, for the purposes of mindfulness, we encourage you to pick breathwork that helps you and your baby to take breaths that promote calm.

The Basics: Diaphragmatic Breathing

This is where it all begins. This is the belly breathing your baby is doing that, somewhere along the way, we forgot how to do as adults. So let's get back there.

1) Place your hands on your stomach.
2) Now, slowly inhale *into your hands.*

3) Focus on letting your breath visibly move your hands out as you breathe in and move in as you exhale.
4) Pay attention to your shoulders and upper chest. More often than not, that's the area we breathe with, and with each inhale our shoulders and chest go up. See if you can keep those muscles still and *instead get your belly to puff out.*

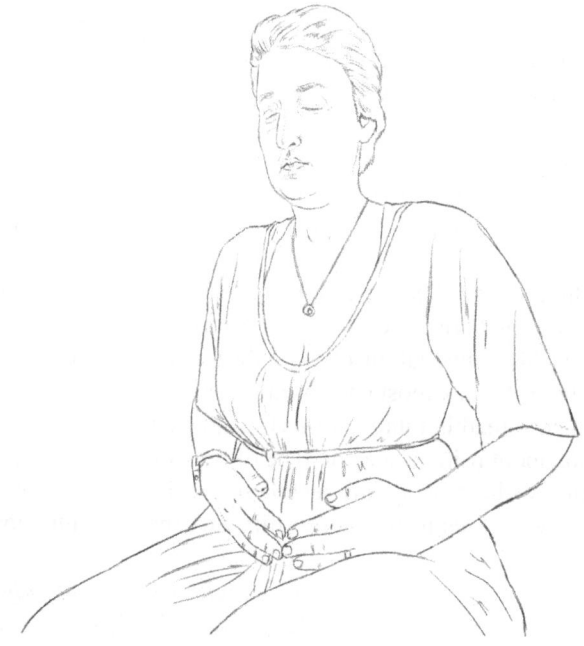

Diaphragmatic Breathing technique.

Now that you know what diaphragmatic breathing looks and feels like, you can do it without your hands to help guide you. While you are snuggled with your little one, simply focus on taking those sweet belly breaths in and out, in and out.

It's surprisingly difficult, so don't get frustrated if you get tired from taking such deep breaths. With practice, you will find the breath becomes easier and even enjoyable.

In the beginning work toward taking six diaphragmatic breaths in thirty seconds.

That seems totally doable, right? It is, and your body will thank you for it. One study showed that you can get benefits, like lower stress and an improved sense of well-being, from just that little amount of deep breathing![1]

Diaphragmatic breathing is your foundational practice. It's the batch of brownies fresh out of the oven. Brownies all by themselves are the perfect dessert. But you *can* add chocolate chips or frosting if you want to make it a little bit more delicious. So if you want to add to your breathing practice, here are some exercises, some chocolate chips and frosting so to speak, that you can use in conjunction with your diaphragmatic breathing.

Technique #1: Ujayi Breathing

Ujayi, also known as victorious breath perhaps because it can sound a bit like a cheering crowd, is accomplished by slightly tightening your throat to create a soft noise with each breath. Constricting your throat to create the "victorious" sound causes vibrations in the larynx that stimulate receptors that tell the vagus nerve—that part of your nervous system that regulates the parts of your body that you do without conscious input (like your heart!)—to go into rest and relax mode. The constriction also pushes slightly on the carotid sinuses in your neck, the part of your body that monitors blood pressure, which encourages it to lower your heart rate. The rhythmic sound of the breath, like waves in the ocean, also promotes a sense of calm and relaxation.

Steps 1 and 2 are "training wheels" to help you learn how to practice ujayi. You can skip them once you feel comfortable.

1) Open your mouth and take a loud, deep breath in and out. Don't engage your vocal cords, but exhale with enough force that it's a very audible breath in and out.
2) Now continue breathing like that but close your mouth. Don't let any air in through your mouth as you inhale or exhale.

You should now be making a noise, almost Darth Vader-esque, from the inside of your throat.

Don't tighten your throat or force the noise. This is actually a very relaxed breathing technique so if you're straining, stop right away and try again from the beginning.

3) Once you feel you're able to comfortably make the ujayi sound without straining, you can practice the ujayi breath without the extra step of opening your mouth.

Ujayi Breathing technique.

Once you get the hang of it, use ujayi breathing whenever, wherever. Snuggle up with your little one on your chest and practice or when you need to regulate before picking them up after they refuse to nap.

This is one of the most versatile breathing techniques and you can do it as much or as little as you like. There's no limit to how long you can indulge your body with these generous breaths.

Technique #2: Alternate Nostril Breathing

A 2013 study found that alternate nostril breathing significantly lowered factors such as heart rate, respiratory rate, and blood pressure[2]—three factors that are directly related to stress, anxiety, and well-being. When these three slow down, it will also help slow down you and your baby. This technique is a perfect activity while nursing, rocking, or other times when you only have one hand free. You can use whichever hand is free—or whichever you prefer.

1) *Extend your thumb and pinky fingers (like the surfer's "hang loose" sign) and bring your hand to your nose.*

2) *Press your thumb to one nostril and create a nice tight seal. Leave your pinky finger extended and your other nostril clear.*
3) *Exhale slowly. Inhale slowly. (Remember to use diaphragmatic breathing!)*
4) *Release your thumb.*
5) *Press your pinky finger down (so that you are closing your other nostril)*
6) *Exhale. Inhale.*
7) *Release your pinky. Press your thumb.*
8) *Exhale. Inhale.*
9) *Continue for as long as you wish.*

Alternate Nostril Breathing technique.

You might find that one side is stuffier than the other side. That's okay, this exercise can help relieve that.

Technique #3: Bumblebee Breathing

This is a phenomenal exercise to do when you or the baby are feeling anxious or tense. It may feel a little strange if you've never done it before. Maybe not the kind of thing you want to do when your parents are over (although if you all did it together, you'd get a really Zen thing going!).

It's called bumblebee breathing because, well, you kind of sound like a bumblebee.

As we covered in the "How It Works" section of the "Mantra" chapter (5), vibration is a comforting sensation for babies and adults alike. And with this breathing exercise, you can give yourself and your baby a nice little bumblebee buzz.

This is typically done with two hands but one works just fine if that's all you've got!

1) *With one finger, touch your ear and find the little bump of cartilage that's between your cheek and ear.*
2) *Gently (very gently!) press it down so it covers your ear canal.*
3) *Put your lips together like you are saying the letter "M" (the m part of M not the eh part).*
4) *Keeping your lips closed and your finger holding your cartilage in place, inhale through your nostrils.*
5) *As you exhale, keep your lips closed and make that mmm sound. Your exhale should be one long hum that vibrates through your whole body.*

Bumblebee Breathing technique.

This is a very calming exercise but also very fun! Your little one will watch you with curiosity and delight as you *bzzzz* yourself to bliss. They will also get to experience the vibrations if you are holding them, which they love! Although, keep in mind they may love it a little bit too much, so if you need them to pay attention to something—like feeding—it's better to hold off in case they get distracted.

Technique #4: 4-7-8 Breathing

This is a simple breathing technique that involves counting the seconds of your breathing. Counting allows you to truly slow down and take in those deep breaths without rushing through them. The act of counting your breaths is also a meditation practice that gives your monkey mind something to hold on to, so you can hold onto the present moment instead.

The pattern is:

1) *Inhale* for four seconds
2) *Hold* for seven seconds
3) *Exhale* for eight seconds
4) *Repeat*

4-7-8 breathing has been called the natural tranquilizer for the nervous system, which is probably why it is especially known for helping people sleep. When you or your little one can't seem to fall asleep, give this a try and find out which one of you passes out first!

7

Space

OVERVIEW

The Nurture Method and Space

Stillness: Surround yourself with minimal distractions so you and your baby can focus on each other.

Observation: Notice what in your space impacts you and your baby, such as light and organization.

Intention: Create a space that serves you and your baby and that you can use to intentionally focus on mindfulness.

Our surroundings affect our mind and body, and certain sights, sounds, and scents can trigger relaxation responses. By designing a mindful space with soothing colors, plants, and intentional decor, you can create a haven for connection and calm. This space can support your mindful practices, making it easier to stay present and focused on your little one.

HOW IT WORKS

Unfortunately, this chapter is not going to be about how to turn your home into a calming haven where the world slows down, and you can unwind, recharge, and rediscover your inner peace. In fact, if your entire home looks and feels like a spa, then that probably means you've somehow moved out of your home filled with little feet and dirty diapers and sleepless nights and moved into an *actual spa*.

But let's stick with that spa concept for a moment—what is it that makes a place "a spa"? Is it a spa because you're getting a massage? Well, ask yourself if you would feel like you were in a spa if you got a massage on the side of a busy highway? No, probably not. The space around you is as much a part of the spa relaxation experience as the physical act of the massage is. That's because our mind and body take cues from the space around us. When we walk into a space with relaxing cues—dim lighting, soft music, trickling fountains, lavender candles—our mind knows, *ah, okay, we're in a safe place and it's time to get calm.*

Part of this is biological: certain sights and sounds create autonomic responses. Darkness produces melatonin, a hormone that makes us sleepy (and has some amazing healing properties). Calm music causes our brains to produce alpha brainwaves, the ones that are present when we are relaxed. The scent of lavender has as powerful an effect on the brain as a Valium in reducing anxiety. The sound of water is perceived as a nonthreatening sound by the brain and induces relaxation.

But part of it is psychological: you *know* what a spa looks and sounds like, so you *know* it's time to chill out. It's Pavlov's Spa, if you will. Just like a dog who receives a treat every time the bell rings will eventually begin to salivate merely at the sound of the bell because his brain tells him it's time for a treat, in the same way if you are told enough times that a spa-like atmosphere means you are going to be able to relax, then when you encounter spa-like cues such as candlelight and lavender your brain will tell your body that it is time to relax.

As usual, before scientists could scan our brains or track our pupil dilation, the wise ones of old figured this out. Take Feng Shui, for instance. Three thousand years ago, Chinese philosophers figured out that space had power and that we could arrange our spaces to help balance and harmonize. Some of the basic tenets of Feng Shui are things like, "Remove negative symbolism," and "Maximize natural light." That's a combination of the psychological (negative symbolism) and the biological (natural light).

Or think about one of the old European cathedrals. The millennia-old buildings with their soaring steeples and towering visages, glittering altar and smoky incense are all designed to invoke an experience of awe, wonder, and worship using psychological and biological cues.

Now, apply all of that to your home and specifically to a special space for you and your baby. The techniques provided here start with the biological—things like colors that soothe and plants that comfort. But the psychological is woven into the process. When creating that mindful space, you are setting the intention that a certain area of your home will be a place for *presence*. Just like a spa looks like a spa so you know it's a spa, your mindful space will look like a mindful space so you will know it is a mindful space. You and baby will know that in this corner of the world, things slow down and both of you can be more centered and grounded together.

Remember that the spa experience is more than walking in, though. Just as you go to a spa to get a massage or soak in a sauna, your mindful space is there to help you better connect with your mindful practices. The space alone won't make you and your family find their inner peace. But you will probably find that it makes your practices easier. You might even find that it becomes a favorite spot for everyone in your family because, whether they know it or not, the little changes you make are helping them feel just a little happier.

TECHNIQUES

1. Location

When choosing a space, start small. The goal should not be to make every nook and cranny of your living area a source of peace and centering. As appealing as that sounds, it's also not realistic with little ones.

Instead, choose one area of your home where you can begin to build a space that can promote mindful interactions. Consider the spaces where you and your baby spend a lot of time together. The nursery may seem like the obvious choice—but it's not necessarily the best one! Many families don't have a dedicated nursery, or if they do, it quickly becomes the epicenter of chaos, or, alternatively, they find that they don't end up spending a lot of time there. Rather than select an ideal space, select a "doable" space. Think about what would be most supportive to you and your baby. It might be a space you use often or it might be a space that has room for change and growth. You might pick a spot that has the sunlight you desire or an area with enough room to add a few plants. You might pick the place where you already feel the most comfortable and/or where you spend the most time.

Here are just a few options other than the nursery that would work perfectly for your mindful space:

- A spare room
- The basement
- A patio
- Your bedroom
- The dining room table, where you and your family gather most often
- The living room, specifically the area surrounding your favorite comfy sofa
- An empty corner by a big window

Whatever space you choose is the right one. However you can incorporate some mindfulness into the space is the right way! Now let's take a look at some of those ways.

2. Colors

While the psychology of color is still a developing science, studies have shown that color can influence a child emotionally and physically.[1] For instance, babies have been found to cry more in yellow rooms and to have increased motor activity in a pink room! Adults also have emotional and physiological responses to color, just FYI (a lot of restaurants are painted red because red is shown to induce hunger), but those responses are also influenced by things like personal preferences, culture, and past experiences.

When thinking about colors to add to your space—whether it's painting the walls, bringing in pillows, or adding art to the walls—consider colors that are *cool* and *subdued*. Cool colors have a calming effect on the body and create a more open, relaxed space. Be mindful of how intense the colors are, though. Cool colors can be overpowering and even depressing if they are too dark and strong (think: navy blue, forest green, royal purple). That's why we recommend looking for subdued colors that are soft and light, such as turquoise, slate blue, periwinkle, sage, and tan. Pair this with neutral colors in your decor for an inviting space that will delight you and your family. You can find color swatches to get you started in the companion workbook at NurtureMethod.com.

3. Light

When selecting a mindful space, try to choose an area that has a healthy dose of natural light. Studies have shown that natural light can support better sleep for babies by helping them develop a healthy circadian rhythm, learn better by forming new synapses, and even live better by preventing some diseases. Keep in mind that if your mindful space is also where they sleep, then you will need to invest in some good blackout curtains!

Whether or not you have natural lighting as an option, you can also choose to bring in artificial lighting that will promote growth, health, and relaxation. Avoid halogen lights or exposed light bulbs, which can cause overstimulation and even anxiety in children. Instead choose soft lighting (think: soft-white or daylight bulbs). Consider using a few different lamps instead of one overhead light; that way you can adjust the lighting as needed and your baby doesn't have to stare up at one bright light in the ceiling.

4. Air

If you've got windows, open them up! Not only in the summer, either. Even in the winter, you can crack your window open for a few minutes to let the cool breeze in. Fresh air brings with it a myriad of emotional and physical benefits from reducing stress to energizing the body!

Opening windows helps you and your baby connect with the outside and with nature, which is an important part of mindfulness. Feeling the breeze, hearing birds, smelling fresh cut grass all bring you more in tune with the world around you, which helps you stay present and connected with the here and now.

We already covered the importance of breath in a previous chapter, so it will probably come as no surprise to you that part of deep, healthy breathing is inhaling fresh air. If you live in an area with heavy pollution or near a lot of traffic, you can still make air a part of your mindful space by getting a good filter system instead (keep reading to learn about one of nature's filtration systems). As long as you get the air moving, you get the benefits!

5. Plants

There are so many wonderful reasons to add plants to your little one's mindful space. Not only can they add some beauty, color, and fragrance, but depending on the plant, they can also bring air-cleansing and humidifying powers!

Plants are nature's filtration system. According to a study by NASA, plants can remove up to 87 percent of volatile organic compounds (toxins that can be found in household items like rugs, grocery bags, and inks) every twenty hours.[2] And of course, we all know that plants "breathe in" carbon dioxide and "breathe out" oxygen, helping to fill the room with fresh, clean oxygen for us to take in with those deep diaphragmatic breaths we covered in chapter 6, "Breath."

Plants can also serve as a humidifier, as they release up to 97 percent of the water that they take in! Of course, it would take a lot of plants to do the job of a store-bought humidifier, but the extra help can't hurt.

But wait, there's even more (we told you there were a lot of reasons to love plants). Plants also bring emotional health. Research has proven that indoor plants improve concentration and productivity, reduce stress levels, *and* boost your mood.[3]

You can order plants online, pick them up at a local plant nursery or florist, or (our favorite) get clippings from friends and family. If you're looking for that extra cleaning and humidifying benefit, leafy plants are your best bet. Here are a few to consider:

- Areca Palm

The Areca Palm is a beautiful tree with elegant leaves and a slender trunk. And as an added bonus, it's a low-maintenance plant which allows you to enjoy the serene beauty without the fuss.

- Spider Plant

A charming plant that has delicate white flowers and sprawling, vine-like leaves. It grows quickly, making it easy to propagate, so you can add more around your home or spread the joy and share with others!

- Boston Fern

With its delicate, lacy fronds and ability to thrive in low-light conditions, this elegant fern is not only a beautiful choice for adding texture

and depth to your space, but it will also do well in just about any space in your home!
- Bamboo Palm

A feathery and elegant plant with slender stems and delicate leaves, the Bamboo Palm will make you feel like you're relaxing on a beach. And its slow-growing nature makes it a great option for someone who doesn't have a lot of time to care for a plant.
- English Ivy

Cascading stems covered in intricately shaped leaves, English Ivy lives up to its name and will make you feel like you're living in an English garden. Its ability to thrive in a range of lighting conditions makes it a great choice for any space no matter where your window is (or if you have one at all!).

Don't think you have a green thumb or feel like you don't have time to keep plants alive? It's so much easier than you might think. Look into "self-watering globes"—they are an inexpensive hack for keeping plants alive. Fill them up, stick them in your plant's soil, and walk away. These planters slowly release water over time, so you don't have to remember to do it. Instead of watering plants every day, you can fill up your planter once a week or once every other week. Check out the glass blown self-watering globes or the wine bottle holder.

6. Organization

Clutter makes us crabby. That's just science.

Research has shown that a child's environment can dramatically impact their ability to concentrate.[4] It may not seem like concentration is something that a baby needs to do, but in fact that skill starts early on—like *in the womb* when they start to concentrate on things like light, sound, and color. Talk about a neat and organized space!

Once your baby is on the outside, concentration becomes a lot harder because there are a whole bunch of sights and sounds to compete for their attention. Learning how to concentrate is an important part of their development. They have a lot to do in that first year as they discover their bodies, learn to eat, to crawl, to stand, to walk, to pick things up, and most importantly to learn how to do all the things they're not supposed to. Which is why a mindful space with fewer distractions can help them on their way!

We cover this more in depth in chapter 8, "Play," but it's key to remember that the baby-product industry is an *industry*. Baby registries and advertisements and stores work very hard to make you believe there's about one hundred non-negotiable, must-have, won't-survive-without items for your baby. Once you register for all those, plus get all the free gift boxes from Amazon and Target, plus the hand-me-downs, plus the garage sale finds, plus a few impulse buys from those Facebook ads you keep seeing, it takes work *not* to have every corner of your home filled with baby things.

This isn't the latest Marie Kondo book you picked up, and we're not going to try and teach you how to organize your entire home (if you figure out an easy way to do that with a baby, please contact us immediately!). However, we do have a few recommendations on simple ways to keep yours mindful. Remember that we only want to focus on a small area specifically designated for mindfulness. So don't get overwhelmed trying to do them all, simply apply them to your little space.

- *Keep only six to ten books and six to ten toys out.* Rotate them rather than adding to them.
- *Get a cube shelf or something similar to store items.* By containing everything in a compact area where you and baby can see everything, you'll be encouraged to keep only what's truly essential.
- *Every time a toy or book is used, put it away before taking out the next one.* Yes, you can start good foundational habits of organization and cleanliness at this age!
- *Store additional items in closed space.* Put everything else you don't need immediately accessible in a closet, box, drawer, or even out of the room. Reduce the amount of visible *stuff*.
- *Decorate with intention.* Decor is great! Since you will probably be spending a lot of time in your mindfulness space with your baby, it's nice to have something engaging, beautiful, or comforting to look at. But be careful not to clutter your walls. Consider putting up only one or two pieces of art and one or two shelves with a few items on them.
- *Keep it simple.* Patterns, shapes, and colors are fun and helpful for babies as they grow. But have a few key items with a few simple patterns. Avoid having blankets, bedding, changing table cover, playmat, carpet, lamp shade, wall art, and curtains all with different and loud patterns.

8

Play

OVERVIEW

The Nurture Method and Play

Stillness: Look for ways to play that make room for stillness, that allow for concentration, and provide time for connection.

Observation: Observe your child as you help them observe the world through play. Invite them to use all their senses and then notice how they respond.

Intention: Select simple toys and activities that encourage mindful engagement and presence.

Because infants aren't able to talk or respond, we often don't think about *playing* with them. But they need it! Right from the start, it helps them strengthen their imagination, dexterity, cognitive abilities, language skills, emotional intelligence, confidence, and resilience, just to name a few benefits. Exploring play mindfully can help them explore and discover the world around them.

HOW IT WORKS

Play isn't just for fun! Babies learn through play, and it's essential to their development. However, the American Pediatrics Association tells us something you probably already knew in your gut: that all that wonderful development hinges greatly on how the caregivers around them connect with and relate to them consistently through play. When you play with your baby, you strengthen your bond with them, you model new concepts, you provide a safe setting for learning, you see the world through their eyes, you learn more about them, you improve your communication with them, and (the reason you're here) *you plant the seeds of mindfulness*. How *you* play with your baby will set the tone for how *they* play as children, and how they play as children will set the tone for how they function as adults.

But in the last few decades, we have slowly been moving away from mindful play, swapping our presence out for products. It's not the first time we've seen this phenomenon of moving away from connection and looking to businesses to manufacture things that will do it for us and there's always one common thread: greed. For instance, starting in the 1940s in the United States, there was a shift in attitude toward feeding newborns. Why should mothers nurse their children when *science* could provide a superior product? This became such a prevalent belief that by the early 1970s, over 75 percent of American babies were fed on formula![1] It's important to stop here and stress that there is *nothing wrong with formula*. A fed baby is a happy baby, end of story. The point of this example is that companies with a strong vested interest in sales were able to convince society that formula is *better* than breastmilk. Formula, they said, was not only healthier, but also more civilized, more freeing, and more appropriate (it was around this time that breastfeeding in public went out of vogue). In other words, we needed to pay them for something to achieve the best results for both ourselves and our babies.

The same thing is happening with play now—organizations are telling us that we should let *them* teach, engage, stimulate, develop our children. We don't even need to be there; we can turn on the app, the music, the video, the toy for our baby and then walk away because they will be getting the best that science can offer. But as we learned with formula, science is not meant to replace what caregivers can provide but instead should serve to *support* them and their babies. And, perhaps most importantly, companies will always promote what is best for them, not for us or our babies.

Play, like breastfeeding, does not need to be improved upon. Yes, of course, it can be supplemented and there are some things that products will do that we cannot (including keeping them occupied so you can have a few minutes of sanity to yourself!).

However, in most cases, play requires nothing but you and your little one and the world around you. So make time for it. Get on the floor. Explore. Enjoy. Experience the wonder that we as adults rarely get to feel anymore. The time when you get to be with your baby in this way, engaging and playing, is fleeting. You'll cherish and never regret the moments you took to be together, and it does so much toward strengthening your bond together.

TECHNIQUES

1. Make Toys Intentional

Without a doubt, toys are an essential part of play! But these days, most toys are focused on distraction rather than growth and learning. Sometimes we need our kids to be distracted. There's absolutely nothing wrong with that. Other children, the dishes, or our own mental health require our attention, and we need to keep our kid occupied for a little while. But pure distraction, just like sugar, should be an occasional treat. Luckily, there are some simple steps you can take to bring mindfulness to the choice of toys that make up a big part of their lives.

Hit unsubscribe

The moment you find out your baby is on the way, the ads, newsletters, websites, blogs, apps, Instagram accounts, Facebook pages, you-name-it will be clamoring for your attention and telling you what you *need* to keep you and your baby happy. But as we discussed, the reality is that most of these recommendations are actually about sales and not about what you or your baby need. In fact, you and your baby need *very* little. Make a conscious decision not to follow, like, subscribe, and download all the baby-related content you come across. Choose one or two reliable sources and let the rest go. Trust your instincts, not advertising.

Minimize toys

You may have a toy store's worth of toys, but instead of bringing them all out, store them out of sight and only keep six to ten toys out at a time. If you already have a lot more toys, rotate them out. We cover this a little bit more in the "Space" chapter (7), too! Toy subscription services can be a great way to keep your toy collection under control and get toys that are perfectly suited for your baby's developmental stage. Tell your friends and family that instead of a toy, you'd like a contribution to the toy subscription service of your choice.

Keep your child's toys:

- *Focused*: When it's time to play, select one toy at a time. When you are done, put it away before taking out the next one. You can teach your baby good habits from day one! And who knows, maybe you will pick up some good habits along the way too?
- *Natural:* Look for items that are made from natural materials like wood, cotton, leather, or wood. Natural toys tend to be:
  - *More environmentally friendly:* Plastic cannot be "sustainably sourced" and most or all plastic parts cannot be recycled.
  - *More durable:* Cheap plastics with stick on decorations will quickly crack, break, and fade. Electronic features quickly break or burn out.
  - *Safer:* Plastic toys are loaded with PVCs, phthalates, or other chemicals. In fact, a 2018 study from the UK found that the plastic in toys made overseas often do not meet current international safety standards.[2] They also tend to have more parts and pieces that can break off, creating sharp edges or choking hazards.
  - *More engaging:* As counterintuitive as that may sound, the more we "spoon feed" our babies with toys that actively try to engage them with lights and sounds, the less engaged they will be. Natural textures stimulate the senses as they invite them to touch, feel, and explore!
- *Quiet*: Yes, stillness is an important part of the entertainment process! Silence provides your child with the opportunity to concentrate on the toy—what it looks like, feels like, sounds like—and also concentrate on the skills it takes to look at and play with the toy. Look for toys that require a skill to make noise (like a rattle rather than something you turn on with a switch). And when you play with the toy, talk with them about it but then also make room for silence so they can take it all in!
- *Simple:* Choose toys that are gentle in appearance. Simple design, simple colors, simple patterns are more than enough for your little one. Much like silence, it is in the simplicity that they can find the

space to learn how to entertain themselves and become engaged with the world rather than requiring the world to engage and entertain them.
- *Unplugged:* Give your baby a chance to learn how to be entertained without the toy doing the entertaining for them! Look for toys that come without plugs or batteries. You may be surprised at how difficult that task can be. So if you're not able to do it, remember that the lights and sounds and other electronic options are just that—an option! Leave the batteries out or keep it unplugged and leave it up to you and your baby to figure out how to have fun with it.
- *In the family:* Ask your family, friends, and neighbors to share a favorite toy that is no longer being used. Often, they are grateful to give an outgrown toy to a loved one. You, in turn, save money, help protect the environment from waste, get a toy that has been kid tested and approved, and can enjoy having a piece of your community to share with your little one. When you take it out, tell baby who it is from, "Here is your cousin's favorite ball!"

2. Play with Your Words

Is talking to your baby a form of play? Sure it is! They sure seem to be having fun when they talk, don't they? You can too, as you explore the world verbally with them. At the same time, talking with them is also a mindful practice as we covered in the technique in chapter 3, "Words." It brings us into the moment with our child by helping us focus on them.

Sometimes we forget to talk to our babies. Like, *really* talk to them, not just the cutesy baby stuff. We usually forget for a good reason—they can't talk back! But even if they're not joining in on the conversation, they *are* listening! They're always listening and learning. Talking to your baby is an important part of their developmental process. It helps their brains grow and can help them do better at school when they're older.[3] The words we use, the sound of our voice, the expressions we make, the connection of our eyes with theirs, they're soaking it all up like little sponges.

Here are a few ways you can use talking to engage with your baby:

- Talk about what they are experiencing around them ("Can you hear the train whistle?" "Look at that green leaf! Do you like that color?")

- Tell them what you will be doing ("I'm going to nibble on your toes now!")
- Process what has just occurred ("What did that feel like? Did it tickle?")
- Chant a mantra (chapter 5)
- Sing a song (chapter 4)

Don't feel the need to use "baby talk" all the time. Mirroring their baby noises and saying things in a cute voice is a part of the communication puzzle with babies, but it's not the only part. Go ahead and use your big ole grown-up words too. This helps build the connection between the words and their actions. Children are so much smarter than we give them credit for!

Remember to incorporate stillness into your talking. When you talk to them, wait for them to talk back! They might not do it, but that doesn't mean they're not trying!

3. Engage the Senses

We are quick to teach our children their "heads, shoulders, knees, and toes" but often forget to teach them what to do with all those tools! Taste, touch, smell, sight, and hearing are five of our best friends when it comes to mindfulness. They guide us back to the present moment, to what is happening right here and right now, and they help us stay connected with our body, something that becomes increasingly difficult as we spend most of our lives as disembodied personalities on our computers and phones.

Babies come out of the womb with their senses, well, infantile but very much engaged. It is so simple and fun to help them explore their new sensory powers!

Sight

So often, we carry baby around, put them in the crib, set them on the playmat, and never stop to explore our surroundings with them. We, as adults, tend to only do that when we're on vacation, soaking in the beaches of Bora Bora or posing in front of Times Square and taking it all in for the first time. Well, guess what? That's exactly what your baby is doing! From the big mug of coffee in your hand to the weeds growing in your neighbor's lawn, everything is one big trip to Bora Bora and Times Square.

What an amazing gift to us, to be able to see the world again through new eyes. Literally.

As you go through your day, see what you can explore visually with your baby.

Bring everyday objects closer to them: What is within reach that you can show them? Everything is up for grabs. Literally! If they are sitting in your lap or going for a ride in a carrier, pick up a boring, everyday object—a plant, a shirt, a picture, a cup—and let them see it. You may find it's not so boring or everyday to them!

Bring them close to objects: Take them on a tour of your home or whatever space you're in. If you've decorated their nursery with beautiful art on the wall, why not show it to them? Bring them into the shower and let them see all the shampoo bottles or stare at the tile wall. Try to see spaces with new eyes as you explore with them. Something you might gloss over as an adult could be fascinating to baby eyes that have never seen it before.

Give them new angles to explore: Once they are on the move, you won't be able to stop them from seeing the world from any angle they can crawl or climb to. But it's up to you to show them all that our three-dimensional world has to offer. Hold them up so they can look out a window, bring their stroller underneath a tree so they can see the leaves rustle, lay them on a blanket in the park so they can watch people's feet as they walk by. Invite your inner child to be curious about the world and what it looks like and bring your baby along with you!

It's helpful to keep track of your baby's developing vision to learn how far they are able to see. Apps like the Wonder Years and BabySee will often show you exactly what your baby is able to see. As you show them all the world has to offer, incorporate both talking and silence. Discuss what you are showing them, ask them what they think about it, and then allow for silence so they can concentrate.

Sound

The sounds of our world are mostly just "white noise" to us grownups. But for your baby, all those noises are a symphony, and each new experience helps their sensory neurons strengthen and develop. Exploring sound with your baby can help them learn about the world, but it can also help you learn about them. You may discover noises that they find calming or enthralling or hilarious.

Observe everyday sounds: As you move about your day, as you sit for a feeding, as you push them in the stroller, pay attention to what sounds you can notice with your baby. Can you listen in wonder to the noise of the air conditioner, the rumble of a lawn mower, the titter of a bird, the honk of a car horn? We've learned to tune them out, but can you tune them back in so you can help your baby experience them? When you notice a noise, talk to your baby about it. Tell them what it is, ask them what they think about it.

Bring them closer to a sound: When possible, bring them closer to the noise. When you turn on the dishwasher, stop and lean in, giving them a moment to allow them to take in the low thrums of the machine at work. Is it raining outside? Head to the window or open the door and let them hear the patter of water falling from the sky and hitting different objects. Does your floor squeak in a certain spot? Next time you walk over it, pause and lower them to the ground so they can hear that squeak that will one day be the bane of their existence when they try to sneak in after curfew. Just like you visually explored things from a new angle, you can do that with sounds too! Let them hear it from near and far. From high then from low.

Create sounds: You are not just at the mercy of the sounds around you. Think about what sounds you can create. We're led to believe that we have to buy toys that rattle, jingle, and crinkle. But the reality is, the world around us makes all those noises even better!
- Bring your face close to theirs and whisper softly.
- Blow air gently near their ears.
- Rap your knuckles on their crib.
- Tap a utensil on a glass.
- Repeat a mantra (chapter 5).

Touch

Rocking them to sleep, carrying them while we do chores around the house, blowing raspberries into their bellies, kissing their cheeks—there's a window of time, both precious and overstimulating, where it seems like we are in constant contact with our littles. But how often is that touch done with mindful intention? Mindful touch can be a fun way to engage with your baby while helping them learn about the many parts and pieces that make up their whole selves!

Gentle sensation: Wet a paper towel and place it on the baby's cheek. During tummy time, run your fingers along their back in different patterns. Blow air across different parts of their body. Tickle them with a blade of grass.

Play games: Remember the game This Little Piggy Went to Market? That little rhyme is more than just a game, it's a teaching tool! Even at this age, we can use touch and words to help our children engage their senses and make connections to what is happening in their bodies.

Some other games that employ touch as a tool include:
- *Head, Shoulders, Knees, and Toes (gently tap each body part as you speak or sing)*
- *How Big Is Baby? (Ask the question and then lift their arms up as you answer, "So big!")*
- *Clapping (Clap their hands or feet to a song or mantra)*
- *The Wheels on the Bus (Move their bodies to the motions in the song)*

Naked time: If you are in a safe and warm place, let it all hang out! Grab an old towel and lay it in the crib or playard, and give your little one a chance to feel the world without onesies or diapers. Clothing-free time allows for full body sensory integration, something they need.

Energy medicine or massage: If you've tried energy work with your baby (chapter 12), you may have already discovered the smiles and giggles that can come with it. Both energy medicine and massage let you and baby play with touch together in a positive way. As you place your hands on different parts of the body, discuss them with your baby: name the different parts, ask how it feels, describe what you are doing. And then make room for silence so they have space to process the information coming in.

Taste

Just because they can't eat, doesn't mean they can't taste! Your baby has been tasting since they were in utero! Taste is such an intense sense that in the NICU, doctors and nurses will give newborns small doses of oral sucrose to help them feel calm and comforted (essentially a spoonful of sugar to help the medicine go down)!

You should never feed your child solid foods until you get the okay from your pediatrician, but it is safe—and fun—to let your baby experience flavors! Never give them more than a drop (until it's time to introduce solids) and remember that honey and unpasteurized foods are off the table!

Here are a few ways to play with the sense of taste:

Rub one drop on their lips: Eating an apple or ice cream? If a little bit gets on your fingers, dab it on their lips.

Give them a tasty kiss: Enjoying a glass of orange juice or a bowl of cereal? What better way to share the yummy flavors than with a kiss!

Baby-led weaning: When you begin solids around six months, baby-led weaning (BLW) is a playful, natural way for your baby to begin their eating adventure.

A LITTLE MORE ON BLW

With BLW, you allow your baby to feed themselves soft chunks of food instead of spoon-feeding them purees. As long as your six-month baby can sit up and grab toys, they are also able to feed themselves and there are numerous benefits for feeding them in this way. Research supports that it helps develop babies' hand-eye coordination, dexterity, and chewing skills. And it could help your little one gain confidence as she explores taste, textures, colors, and smells on her own.

Another big draw is that it helps to develop healthy eating habits, as the baby stops eating when they are full as opposed to when they are spoon fed. Also, many babies who are fed this way become more adventurous eaters who are more open to trying different tastes and textures.

Downfalls are the mess, as a lot of the food does not make it to their mouth—especially at first—and you don't know exactly how much they are eating. But feeding at six months is all about experimentation anyway, since babies are still getting most of their nutrients from breastmilk or formula up until one year. So it's definitely worth a try—as long as there are no concerns—check with your doctor if you're unsure at all.

The best part of this method may be that your baby eats at the same time, at the same table, and shares the same food as the rest of your family. Family mealtimes are a great way to develop togetherness and bonding and nourish your baby as she grows into toddlerhood, childhood, and beyond.

Smell

Newborns arrive with a highly developed sense of smell. So developed, in fact, that they can smell their mothers from one to two feet away! Just one more reason why you may not be able to sneak away when they're sleeping.

Play with that ability and watch their eyes widen as their brain goes to work. Always be gentle when introducing new smells, and don't force anything so close that they can't turn their head away if the smell is unpleasant or overwhelming to them.

Note: It is best to stay away from scented candles and air fresheners, which usually rely on chemicals. When exploring scent, stick with natural smells.

Bring new smells to them: Open your spice cabinet and pick out a spice for them to sniff. Peel an orange and let them smell the rind. Hold up fresh, clean laundry and let them take a sniff.

Bring them to new smells: A flower, the grass, the bubble bath you're about to enjoy.

Aromatherapy: Pick up some scented oils and you can both enjoy the benefits. Lavender and chamomile are two calming scents that can even help baby sleep! *Note: Never put undiluted essential oils on a baby's delicate skin.*

4. Facetime

No, not that kind! We're talking about old-school facetime. Do you know what your baby likes to look at more than anything?

Your face.

So allow them to be close to you, near your face, and just let them explore. It's so fun for them to be so close to you and touch all those parts. As you hold their hand to your eyes, you can say eyes and nose as they touch your nose. It's all so new to them and so much fun to be so close to that face that they adore more than anything. Almost all of the senses are at play when you are this close, and it's pure joy for your little one.

Looking in the mirror is another way to experience facetime. They may still be working out that they are the other person in the mirror but they'll definitely recognize you! You will see them light up as you make silly faces, laugh, and smile into the mirror together. You can use a mirror during tummy time to keep them entertained as they work on developing those new muscles and skills. You can even use it for teaching them different parts of the face as you point to your eyes, nose, and mouth. Or show them the different emotions with your happy, sad, surprised, scared, and angry faces. As you know, they pick up so much even before they use words, so hearing these words early on can only help their language development. Dr. Rochat from Emory University developed the five stages of awareness for babies:[4] "That's a mirror (Level 1), there's a person in it (Level 2), that person is me (Level 3), that person is going to be me forever (Level 4), and everyone else can see it (Level 5)." So not only is it fun and super simple because you likely already have one in the house, but it also helps to develop their self-awareness.

9

Adventure

OVERVIEW

The Nurture Method and Adventure

Stillness: Look for moments of quiet in the midst of your experiences and adventures and practice being present and still.

Observation: Notice and call out all that you and your baby are experiencing in the moment, what do you see, touch, smell, hear, and feel? Open and allow for wonder and curiosity to unfold.

Intention: It may not be new for you, but it is for your baby. Approach the world with the intention of seeing it through the eyes of a child.

Embracing adventure involves seeing the expected and unexpected moments of the day with a sense of curiosity and wonder. With curiosity, we stay open to possibilities and see setbacks as opportunities for growth. Anything can become an adventure when you approach it from the lens of making it fun and finding the awe in it. Adventurous activities with your little one, such as storytelling, reading, and exploring, are powerful tools that build bonding, literacy, and emotional intelligence. They also boost mood, incorporate exercise, and foster a respect for nature. By embracing these tools, you'll not only nurture your child's sense of awe but also rekindle your own, making parenting a journey of discovery and joy.

Chapter 9

HOW IT WORKS

What is adventure except facing challenges, taking risks, and exploring the unknown? For your baby, *everything* is an adventure. Every day is a call for them to step into undiscovered territory and courageously do something different and new. For you, it may not always feel that way. In fact, it's natural to feel some sadness over the changes from letting go of what life was before baby and embracing what life is now. It's a grieving process like any other as you close one chapter and open another. You may have less free time, yet you may find yourself using time differently, appreciating it even more now that you have so much less time to yourself. You may feel a lack of freedom with the arrival of this little being who is dependent on you for everything. You can't spontaneously come and go as you please, as you once did. Mindfulness gives us the opportunity to approach each day with an intention of meeting that curiosity and wonder, allowing you to feel the spark of excitement within you too. Adopting an attitude like this takes away some of the monotony you may feel when you're at home with your little one.

A mindfulness reframe like this enables you to see things a little more like your baby does, with that same sense of wonder. Your day-to-day experiences may not seem like adventures from the point of view you had before you had children. Yet once you're in it, you'll be in awe as your little one grows right before your eyes and you find yourself doing really hard things, pushing yourself, simply out of love for your little one. As you use your mindfulness practices to stay open to the changes that will inevitably happen, instead of clinging to what was or how it used to be, you'll find a greater level of awareness, connection, and flow in your journey during this life change.

By reframing any feelings of limitation with the intention of uncovering the wonder and awe in your new experience, you positively impact the way you live and view your life. Knowing that your perceived limitations don't hold you back is a virtue that will transcend parenting, and your baby will eventually pick up on it, too. Challenges help you grow, and with a child, there will be many. The more you see these challenges as opportunities to grow, the greater enjoyment, gratitude, excitement, and joy you'll find along the way.

The Benefits of Awe and Wonder

Adventure comes with a whole host of benefits. Research shows that babies benefit from adventures because they are experiences that stimulate their sense of wonder and awe.[1] By incorporating adventures into your daily routine, you nurture curiosity and encourage exploration for you and your baby, which contributes to their cognitive development.[2] Keep in mind that adventure is more than physical activity. It is any journey of discovery that stimulates your physical, mental, and emotional well-being while enhancing problem-solving and sparking creativity.

Bring On the Good Vibes

A positive vibe will be felt in your home as you embrace the unknown with an attitude of acceptance and making it fun—just like when you embark on a new adventure. There are plenty of physical and psychological health benefits that come from incorporating adventures into your day. By creating time for exploring, indoors and out, physically and mentally, you can boost your mood, integrate exercise and movement, soak up some much-needed vitamin D (but don't forget about sun safety, and grab the sunblock and hats too), build brain power, allow for openness and expansion, plus it's totally free.

Taking on adventures of any kind can even provide intellectual stimulation including problem-solving, cause and effect, and STEM education while improving your family's overall level of well-being. And you are teaching your little one to treat our world with respect as you venture out into it and take care of it.

When you can't figure out the source of your baby's troubles, go out for a walk, lie on a blanket in the grass, bundle up and look at the night sky. Inside can be boring *and* overstimulating. Being outside nearly always settles a crying baby.

So don't let bad weather or the fact that you live in the city or don't want to get dirty or that you are not creative hold you back from getting out and having an adventure. Whether it's one you create through a story or imaginative play in your living room or outside in a green space, it's never too early to start exploring. It will make your days more fun and plant seeds for all the adventures that are sure to come as your family evolves.

We'll look at two ways you can approach adventure: physically (exploration) and mentally (storytelling).

TECHNIQUE

Stories

What better way to go on an adventure than with a story? Stories captivate us and also teach us lessons, boost our moods, deliver truths, and open up new worlds as you imagine yourself stepping into the life and perspective of the character you are learning about. Stories, either ones you read or create yourself, are a great way to sprinkle Nurturing practices into your baby's life.

In storytelling, you and your baby are not only experiencing an adventure, but it can also help improve your mood and help you process life situations. According to Paul Zak, PhD, a neuroeconomist, a good story is "one that captures us, moves us, transports us." He shares that the act of storytelling offers benefits to both the teller and listener. It even triggers the "[secretion of] oxytocin, the neurochemical known for its ability to promote bonding," among other positive results.[3]

Storytelling is one of the best tools for parents, because it's always there, ready to be put to use. You don't have to wait to be around the campfire, you just need your imagination, which is always at the ready. Stories can make everyday experiences more fun for you and your babies. Having fun often leads to laughter, and you know the enormous health benefits of that. And on some days when you're at home with little ones, being able to laugh about it may be your only ticket for staying sane. You see, babies and children under the age of five are all energy and emotion. Logic doesn't even begin to develop until around the age of five. Creative storytelling is one way to connect with them, spark their curiosity, foster their imagination, and lighten everyone's mood.

Read aloud

It's easy to think that because your baby can't speak that they can't enjoy listening to stories, but you can start reading to your baby from the moment they arrive and they will *love* it! Reading aloud to your little one is about more than just literacy. Books transport children on amazing adventures that help with their development of vocabulary, comprehension, listening skills, focus, and even help with connecting and bonding.

You don't even need to do the reading if you don't want to. Instead of listening to music, you can play a podcast story or an audiobook. There are so many to choose from—everything from fairy tales to Greek mythology to the classics—they're out there. So set up that Audible account or get hooked up with your library, which offers audio versions of anything you fancy or think your little one might. If all else fails, try "Alexa, tell us a bedtime story," and you'll discover that your Amazon Alexa app churns out a good story too.

Get creative

You don't have to stick to stories that other people have written. You can create your own stories that are there for you anytime! Creative storytelling is one of the best tools for parents, because it's always there, ready to be put to use. The sky's the limit when it comes to creative storytelling. Tap into your childlike wonder and let your imagination run wild. It doesn't have to follow a traditional story arc or be anything complex—it just has to be whatever you dream up, however simple or silly it may seem.

Incorporate stories into your day

As babies get older, you'll find that when you rattle off instructions or ask them to do things, it often goes in one ear and out the other. They don't get it; they don't connect to it.

But turn it into a story, make it fun, add some rhythm to it. Then it works. You know you know how to do it. You've seen those parents spooning their baby's food by pretending it's an airplane zooming around or chugga-chugga-choo-choo-ing until the food makes its last stop in their baby's mouth. Or a parent zooming their little one around the living room like superwoman before she soars into the tub for her bath. That's creative storytelling, and parents do it because it works. Here's an example of how you could bring storytelling into your day:

"Well, my little fairy friend, it's almost lunch time. Here, let me sprinkle fairy dust all over you with my magic wand [as you tickle baby gently and get a little giggle] so we can put away your toys extra speedy before we head into our fairy house's little kitchen for lunch. Sweet potatoes, smashed peas . . . yum, yum, yum, yum. You tell me all about it as we change that little diaper of yours [as you pretend to fly baby over to the changing table and continue the story, sharing more about the adventures you will go on as you change baby's diaper]. Alright, you have a fresh diaper and your very best pixie wings, now let's get you lunch before you have to fight that dragon [more kisses and cuddles and giggles as you share how grateful you are that your baby is so brave and able to protect you both]."

Adding an accent only helps matters! It may seem silly, but it becomes even more useful when you are working with a toddler. You can tap into this creative storytelling craft and plug right into their imagination. What does your baby want more than anything? Your attention. A story makes them really tune in and connect with that precious attention you are giving them. And when a child feels love and attention, they are less likely to make that not-so-great choice or bubble into that huge tantrum. It diverts them toward something positive, fun, and a little adventurous or outside the norm.

Process

When your baby gets older, you will often find them reenacting parts of their day in their play. Did they get a shot at the doctor? You'll be playing doctor and receiving several hundred shots before the week is over. That's because children often process the world around them through storytelling. So if your child experiences something new, difficult, or interesting, you can help them (and perhaps yourself too) better understand it through stories.

Go beyond baby books

You're not limited to "age-appropriate" books! An infant can enjoy *Much Ado About Nothing*, *The Little Prince*, or *The Neverending Story*, too. Use this as an opportunity to return to classics you once loved. With whatever you are reading, they get to hear new words, listen to your voice (don't forget to act out the different characters!), see words on a page, and spend time snuggled up with their favorite person. If you have other children, you don't have to read to each child separately.

This will evolve as your baby grows and you create a cherished family read aloud time. There is a good reason why Storytime is an activity you can find for you and your baby at coffee shops, libraries, and other community spots. It's an escape, an adventure, and it's fun!

Of course, look for books that have a message and content that you are comfortable sharing with your baby. Even though they cannot understand everything, babies pick up on a lot, including the energy you give off. So, perhaps leave the true crime novels or any other highly disturbing topic for adult-only time.

Pick simple over exciting

While those epic novels can be fun to sprinkle in, the story you tell doesn't have to be long and complicated. Remember, even the simplest stories are an adventure in the eyes of your baby and helpful for their language development.

Many children's books have given into the distraction attraction we talked about in chapter 8, "Play." But if you look at the classics, like *Pat the Bunny*, *The Very Hungry Caterpillar*, or even books by Dr. Seuss, you'll notice they have something in common. Simple drawings often surrounded by lots of white space. In this simplicity, you and your child have the room to concentrate and truly look at, appreciate, learn about the images, and connect to the characters.

Choose your own adventure

Do you remember those books where you could choose which path your character went on? It's a good concept that is important as you choose what books you read to your little one. When you choose a book for your child, make sure it feels good to you. That might seem like an odd instruction. Are there children's books that feel good to parents? Shouldn't it be what feels good for the child? Yes. But what feels good for the parent also feels good for the child. If you enjoy a book, if the pictures are beautiful to you or the story amuses you or the lesson resonates with you, that will impact the experience for both of you. Don't force yourself to read a book that you hate. Give that one away and make room in your book rotation for something special that delights you.

Reinforce your values

You can use stories to teach important lessons and values, while also fostering a lifelong love of reading, curiosity, and an appreciation for different cultures.

Once your little one is able to bring their hand to their mouth (around two to three months) and then transfer hand to hand (five to seven months), game on. They explore objects with their mouth. Hence those brilliant indestructible books that can be gummed, folded, thrown, you name it and it survives. Aside from the indestructibles, you can use books to teach gentleness. Modeling the right way that books should be treated is a great practice. They're not food, and they're not toys. If your baby tries to chew on a book, verbally remind them, "Books are for reading" and then replace the book with a toy or teether.

Teaching them to respect their own things leads to them learning how to respect others' things and the world we live in. It's never too early to instill this value of responsibility and respecting self and others, and this may be one of the first ways to plant that seed.

Find magic

Is there magic in the world? If you have an imagination, then the answer is yes! Many adults have lost sight of magical thinking because we don't need it as much as we get older. Becoming a parent changes that.

Connecting to children's innate sense of awe by getting there yourself is one of the best ways to connect with them, get messages across, and help to teach principles and values. If you're using your imagination, you're speaking children's language.

Allow yourself to be imaginative, playful, and fun. Not just for your baby, but for you too! From getting ready for bed to battling through tummy time, creative storytelling can help you move through daily activities with a hint of adventure, bringing new and uplifting words to you and your baby, and making even mundane activities more exciting.

Exploration

Inside

From choosing the theme of the nursery to deciding between the woodland or outer space–themed playmat, you are creating little adventures for your baby all the time without even knowing it. Remember, everything is new to your little one and you don't need to do or show them much to spark their attention. Don't be afraid to take a moment to explore. Let them look, feel, touch what is in their environment. If you're moving too fast, you both may miss it.

Once your baby starts moving and interacting more with their environment, you can create a lot of fun right in your own home or backyard. Here are some ideas to get you started, but the possibilities are endless. Allow your imagination to soar, and see how the most unlikely things can feel like an adventure for your little one:

- *Boxes.*
  Don't bring those Melissa & Doug boxes out to recycling yet. As soon as your baby can sit, a box suddenly turns into something fun to touch and explore. Incorporate it into peek-a-boo or place their rattle inside to see if they can find it. Since everything goes into their mouth at this age, you'll not want to leave it around for too long. As they get older, boxes can become part of a story you are reading or imaginative play by turning it into a pirate ship, spaceship, or puppet theater that may stay around a bit longer than was possible with your wee little one.
- *Sensory engagement.*
  Babies learn by connecting with you and what they are feeling and experiencing around them with their senses. Engaging their sense of hearing is fun when you use rattles, bells, or anything they can shake or bang (kitchen measuring cups, spoons, and spatulas work well here). Moments of silence and your own singing is even good for this aural development. As they begin moving, having a nice contained, soft space to move around, touch, and explore is great for them and you (so you know it is safe and don't have to worry). Maybe include a bin of soft balls and blocks that they can touch and mouth and feel as they roll or slither around. Fill a bin with water and let them scoop and play. The same kind of play at bath time makes it so much fun. Don't rush it. Let them enjoy and play in there (as you are watching and do it in a way that is safe for them, of course!). Let them sit in or put their feet on different surfaces like the grass, sand, dirt, smooth rocks—whatever is available—while keeping an eye on them to not get a mouthful of it. All

of these sensory experiences are opportunities for exploration and offer super fun and learning for your little one.
- *Cause and effect.*
  Cause and effect is a fun phenomenon to explore. You can use blocks and create a tower that they can knock down. Or you could place little bells on their ankles. As they move their feet, they will hear the sound. Tie a balloon from a string onto their ankle and let them feel and see what it is like to hit it with their hand or foot and see how the balloon moves when they do. Fill old plastic water bottles with different materials like dyed water, beans, pom poms, pipe cleaners (and make sure they are secured shut). Then, let them play with them and see what happens as they knock them down and explore the different weights. This is why peek-a-boo and hide-and-seek are so fun for them. Throw up a scarf or bandana and then watch them fall, or hide one in a toy and let them discover where it is and find it again. Consider these their first science experiments!

This is a good place to remind you that you are not seeking perfection. Don't focus on creating a scene that looks good on social media. This is all about creating opportunities for exploration. Don't feel discouraged if it looks a little messy or not as neat as it did for that person you follow on Instagram. The moment thoughts like that creep in, you lose your presence, you are not in the moment with your baby. They don't care that it looks just right. Remember that core ingredient? They just want you to be there with them, mirroring the excitement and awe they feel. Embark on these little adventures at home knowing it's your being with them that makes any experience most fun for them.

Outside

Adventuring outside your home with your little one is fun too. At first, this may just be a walk. Believe us, your first walk will feel like an adventure (check out "Rituals" in chapter 10 for more on making your first outings go smoothly). It won't be long until you're up for more than a walk around your neighborhood. Next, it may be a nearby nature preserve or conservatory, a trail, the zoo, or a nearby park.

Having a child helps you get out and explore areas and places that you might not have ventured to before they arrived. Having a child takes you out of your comfort zone. You tend to be more open to trying something new because you are creating new experiences for them. And let's face it, experiencing things yourself again through their curious and awestruck eyes brings a lot of joy.

Some of the best adventures are in nature. By taking time to be outside, you nurture a love of the outdoors for your child. We sometimes think we have to be on vacation or in some beautiful space or preserved nature area to really enjoy nature. But you can find ways to explore nature even if it's your own small backyard or next to a busy street in a huge metropolis. You can always find a patch of green space or a park, or you can venture outside your city limits to a forest preserve or trail system. You may have to seek nature out if it's not right outside your door, but that doesn't mean nature isn't available for you. Get creative and make some time for it and see how it provides a host of other benefits to you and your growing little one. Here are a few things to keep in mind:

- *Don't be afraid of dirt.*
  Believe it or not, playing in the mud can benefit your child's sensory development and even their immune system! Let them feel the grass on their toes and dirt beneath their feet. Sit in the sandbox and even make a gooey mud pie. It teaches cause and effect and ignites their creativity.
- *Keep it unstructured.*
  Unstructured outdoor playtime is fun and freeing. Free play has numerous benefits, including relieving stress and anxiety as well as improving cognitive development, social skills, emotional well-being, and creativity. Even if your baby is too young to play and is just watching, this unstructured outside time plants the seeds for you and them. Being exposed to different sights, sounds, and smells is so good for them—they'll feel the energy and enjoy watching all the action.
- *Break out of your comfort zone.*
  Exploring new places can be scary because everything isn't in your control. We do love predictability. But many of life's greatest

joys we couldn't have predicted or had any control of. That is why we need to be open to the unexpected. You learn this acutely once you bring that baby home. Of course, it's more comfortable to do what you've always done than to try something new. It's human nature. Why go on a hike to someplace new when you can take the walk around your neighborhood that you always do? Well, sometimes that familiar place is great and just what you need. But it's also good to go out, explore, and try something new. It's never too early to plant that seed. So go ahead and give yourself permission. Be adventurous and, with your baby as co-pilot, explore something new. If not now, then when?

Having a baby is an adventure in itself. You'll find yourself more vulnerable than you ever imagined, so give yourself some grace and meet yourself where you are. Remember, wherever you are on the adventure scale is exactly where you need to be. Each parent's idea of adventure is unique, so don't be afraid to keep putting yourself out there, trying new things, and embracing that vulnerability. Adventures add fun, excitement, and a touch of discomfort, all essential elements of a rich and authentic life that you want your child to experience too.

10

Ritual

OVERVIEW

The Nurture Method and Ritual

Stillness: Allow the intentional practices of your day to bring you into ease and quiet.

Observation: Notice how your body feels as you fall into the ease of familiar actions of a repeated practice.

Intention: Make a point of choosing something to mean more. Turn a routine act into a ritual that gives you and your baby a mindful moment of connection.

By weaving moments of stillness, mindful observation, and intentionality into your daily routine, ordinary tasks can become sacred rituals. Embracing these moments of focused attention helps to make your days more meaningful while bringing you a sense of ease and comfort. Even on the most chaotic days, returning to your rituals can center you and nurture a deeper connection with yourself and your baby.

HOW IT WORKS

Being home with your baby—especially at first—can put you into all-out survival mode, and your daily activities may feel incredibly mundane as you repeat the same things over and over. But turning the mundane into a ritual is how you can create a Nurturing experience. Babies require a lot of our attention, so creating rituals allows you to carve out small meaningful moments, helping you return to the present and move through tasks with greater intention.

Rituals are to routines as fudge is to a sundae. A sundae without fudge is just ice cream and a routine without ritual is just a schedule. Rituals are what make the everyday into something Nurturing. When a baby comes into our world, so much becomes out of our control, and that can create stress. But it goes beyond simply helping to reduce stress at home. Routines and rituals provide a structure that creates connection and bonding,[1] fosters emotional regulation and resilience (one might call it equanimity), and even strengthens familial relationships and emotional support.[2]

A Remedy for Unpredictability

Babies are kind of like another word for "unpredictable." While routines may fall by the wayside when things go awry, rituals hold deeper significance and might be just what you need to turn things around. You may not be able to give your baby a bath as you intended to, but you can find a way to sprinkle in the ritual by intentionally slowing down, washing away the day with a couple deep cleansing breaths together, and bringing in one of your special practices to connect. See the difference? Rituals are flexible enough to move within the chaos and have the added level of sacred that make them harder to skip over.

There will be times when you'll be sleep-deprived or overwhelmed by the unpredictability and weight of the day and implementing your ritual will not be possible. Remember to give yourself grace. Rituals are not meant to be an added stress. In the early days, simply take a moment to observe daily tasks and see what components felt special or energized you. Then you can set an intention to incorporate it again, once again observing how it felt. Suddenly, a new ritual is formed as you carve it in.

It's Never Too Late . . . or Too Early

As you cultivate these Nurturing rituals, remember that the time to start is right now—whenever now is. Your baby's brain is wired for adaptability and growth. Research shows that children's brains are incredibly malleable, with neural connections forming and reforming at a rapid pace.[3] This adaptability allows them to learn and adjust to new habits and rituals with ease, meaning it is never too early to start planting the seeds of ritual or too late to nurture one in. Right where you are is right where you are meant to be. Now let's look into some ways to incorporate rituals into your day.

TECHNIQUE

Your 3Rs: Routine, Ritual, and Rhythm

R&R is not enough for parents; you need R&R&R, otherwise known as routine, ritual, and rhythm. While the 3Rs seem interchangeable, they have subtle differences, and all play an important role at home with baby. When we discuss routines, we're usually referring to the daily tasks you complete, often in a systematic order, such as baby wakes, diaper change, feeding, and play. Routines are very important for babies and children, because they thrive on predictability and consistency.

Rhythm is, like the name suggests, turning the routine into something musical. When you get into your rhythm, you get into the *groove*. You are no longer marching to the beat; you're dancing to it because you know the steps and you can add your own flair to it. A routine is going for a walk, a rhythm is going for a walk but also making sure you gather your supplies before you go and refilling those supplies when you get back.

Ritual is the mindfulness piece, the intentional act to bring deeper significance. Your ritual is the energy behind what you do. Instilling stillness, observation, and intention into your daily experiences helps you create routines and rhythms that reflects your own family's values. Rituals don't have to be lengthy, sometimes it's just a kiss on your baby's belly each time you finish changing their diaper. They are acts—small or large—that you do, look forward to, and feel some fulfillment from doing. Every day is going to have a mix of moments, some planned, some not, some intentional, some not. By incorporating rituals, you are ensuring there are some intentional, life-giving moments each day.

Think of the 3Rs like the phrase "you can't stop inertia." Once something is set in motion or established, it tends to keep moving in the same manner. And while obstacles will come in your family's way, your 3Rs will keep guiding you back.

Mornings

Mornings are often a baby's best time. At the beginning of the day, they are rested (hopefully), and with the break of a new day and the first sun may come new hope and possibility for you—a feeling that you can do this. You often find them offering their best smiles and giggles at the start of a fresh day. This is a wonderful period to create a special time with you and baby. If you can, open up the shades to welcome the sun. As babies develop their own circadian rhythm, this morning light and activity helps them begin to associate their days with being awake and nights with sleep.

Incorporating your baby into your morning activities can be a beautiful way to create meaningful rituals and make the most of this special time together. Try:

- Wearing your baby while you make breakfast or enjoy a cup of coffee, feeling their warmth and snuggles as you start the day
- Sitting them with you at the table for a meal or snack, watching them take in the brand-new world around them
- Taking a short stroll together, either around the house or outside in a stroller, breathing in the fresh air and enjoying the sights and sounds of nature
- Enjoying some quiet time together, listening to music or doing some gentle movements

Whatever it is that feels good for you, do it. And try to do it consistently, so your baby begins to associate these activities with the morning.

Rest Time

Early on, babies have very short windows of awake time. When your baby falls asleep (even during the day), use this time to make a ritual out of self-care. What do you need during this break? Get still and listen in, your inner voice won't lie. Here are some ideas:

- Take a nap too!
- Take a few deep cleansing breaths, letting go of any tension or stress before you get a few things done
- Put your feet up and indulge in a special cup of tea or coffee, savoring the flavor and aroma
- Stretch your body, either doing a yoga pose or just finding whatever feels good
- Think about how you want to show up between now and the next nap time and an intention for the next part of the day
- Simply sit in silence, enjoying the quiet and stillness of the moment

As nap times become more consistent, it will likely grow into a sacred time for you. Creating a special ritual during this time may give you the boost you need to get through the rest of the day. Make it your own, and make it be what you need to refresh and show up as your best when your little one wakes.

Mealtimes

The practice of family mealtimes can start early, teaching your little one to enjoy food and appreciate the experience. Mindful eating can be lost in busy days, so prioritize mealtimes as a ritualistic activity as best you can. Many people discover they eat healthier when preparing meals for their families, as they have the added intention of nourishing and Nurturing their loved ones.

When at home with a baby, time for food preparation may be limited. Take advantage of offers for food help and stock up on healthy, easy-to-prepare snacks. Babies learn by observing, so model healthy relationships with food with your mealtime rituals.

Even in early feeding stages (breastfeeding or bottle feeding), you're establishing mealtime rituals and Nurturing your baby. To add some ritual to your mealtime, consider sprinkling in something like:

- Say a blessing or express gratitude
- Light a candle (electric ones you can turn on and off quickly are perfect for this!) to create a special atmosphere
- Play soothing music in the background
- Pause between bites: Take a brief pause between bites to breathe, relax, and recharge
- Talk about what you are tasting, how it is, what you look forward

to sharing with them when they can eat too

As babies become more alert and responsive between three to six months, it becomes fun to have them with you and to talk with them as you prepare and enjoy your meals. Tell them what you are making, how you are making it, the colors and methods.

This leads into when they are six months and begin eating some solids—as long as they can sit up by themselves and have strong enough neck control. Of course, they are still getting their nutrients entirely from their breastmilk or formula, but at this point they may start some solids too, and it's such a great time for them to begin the ritual of exploring and enjoying food—the tastes, feels, and smells, all with you!

You may consider baby-led weaning, which entails giving babies soft versions of the foods you are making for yourself. Steamed vegetables and soft fruits in large enough pieces that they can hold and pick them up in their hands and explore fully. You will likely omit the seasonings or tone those down considerably, but it really gives the baby the opportunity to explore tastes, textures, and aromas of a variety of foods. It's messy of course, but a lot of fun. You may choose to give your baby pureed food, another option. If you want to learn a little more about baby-led weaning, head to chapter 8 on "Play" and read the section on playing with the senses.

Bringing a baby into your mealtime may bring more mess and more cleanup, but it brings a lot of fun too. You are starting a ritual that you and your baby will enjoy together for a lifetime. Why not start the ritual early on? Make it something that you can really be present for and share with your child in a positive way.

Tidy Up

You will not be changing diapers, cleaning bottles, or picking up things forever, though some days it may feel like it is all you do. Incorporating a "tidying up" ritual will create a sense of ease and order in your home. It can be hard to find that inner calm if your surroundings are chaotic. A minute here or there can make a big difference. As you establish this ritual, your toddlers will be able to join in when they're ready, and these are valuable skills for them to learn. Plus, as the saying goes, many hands make light work. Working together, you'll all contribute to the process and appreciate the results. Here are some ways to create your "tidy up" ritual:

- *Visualization:* Think of how it will feel when things are sorted and tidy. That visualization may help you take the time to do it now. Describe what you're doing and why, sharing your thought process with your little one.
- *Make it an adventure:* Even cleaning can be fun if you approach it with mindfulness! Invite your imagination to help you with some creative storytelling.
- *Gratitude practice:* Reflect on the things you're grateful for as you put them away, cultivating a sense of appreciation.
- *Be intentional with your time.* You know that saying where solving one problem leads to more problems? Sometimes that can happen with tidying. It can go on forever. Setting a timer is helpful so you don't get caught up and spend the entire nap time cleaning. It also helps you to stay focused on the task of tidying and not get sidetracked doing something else.

Evening/Bedtime

Your evening ritual may be one of the most special of all your rituals. It is said our last thoughts and feelings before sleep are our first as we wake up. So make them intentional for you and your baby through the practice of rituals. In the first weeks, as we have said before, you are just getting used to everything and may be very much in survival mode, so just be patient with this process and yourself. But as soon as it feels right for you and your baby, begin looking for ways to add ritual to your evening.

Baby bedtimes should start as early as 6:00 or 7:00 p.m.—as that is the time the baby will eventually go down when they begin sleeping for more extended stretches and eventually through the night. This allows babies to wake around sunrise, 6:00–7:00 a.m., which aligns with our biological clock and helps establish their natural circadian rhythm.

This is the time when you want to begin removing anything that can be overstimulating for a baby. Try incorporating some of the following rituals into your routine:

- Dimming the lights and closing blinds or shutters to create a peaceful atmosphere
- Playing calming, peaceful music
- Giving baby a bath or a wipe down to release the day
- Getting baby into their pajamas in their sleep space
- Adding a light-touch massage or energy work
- Reading or telling a story (even if baby is too young to understand, it's a great way to start the habit)
- Singing a lullaby or special song

Your bedtime ritual is a practice, and it will take you and your baby some time to adapt to it. However, piecing together the components that feel good for you and consistently doing them with baby in the evening will help them become more sacred and leave you and your baby feeling nurtured at the end of the night.

The time period from around 5:00 p.m.–8:00 p.m., sometimes called the witching hour, can be a fussy time for many babies, especially between zero to three months. It may take a couple months to begin a nighttime ritual as you may be holding and trying to soothe a crying, fussy baby during this time. However, creating the environment for sleep through consistent rituals will certainly help to plant the seeds of a successful nighttime.

Be patient with yourself and your baby in establishing your nighttime ritual. It will not happen overnight. And be sure to create a ritual that feels good to you. If you don't like singing, don't add that part in. If you prefer to give your baby a bath in the morning, that's okay. Observe what sparks joy for you and your baby, and intentionally carve it in.

Getting Out and About

Getting out and about can seem very hard, especially at first. By creating a ritual around it, it can become easier and the next time is easier, then it gets easier still, and suddenly it feels like something you've always done. Here are some practical steps to make your "getting out of the house" ritual more approachable and enjoyable.

Set up

To cut down on stress when going on an outing with your baby, find a moment to yourself when you are in a calm, unhurried state of mind, and think about what you'll need for your trip out into the world. Have your bag packed with everything you need. If possible, keep your bag ready to go—include an extra blanket, spare outfit, bib, pacifiers, burp cloth. Now you've done the routine part. What are some ways you can sprinkle meaning and Nurturing into this by creating a pre-outing ritual, such as:

- Saying a little prayer or mantra for a smooth trip
- Doing a quick meditation or deep breathing exercise
- Putting on a special "adventure" playlist

Do the thing

And you're off! Remember to be compassionate with yourself and your baby. You and your baby will figure out how to explore together soon enough. And whether you're going to the grocery store or meeting friends, you can add a little ritual to your outing. It only takes a second to:

- Note something about your surroundings with your baby, taking a moment to connect with where you are and enjoy it
- Give your baby a kiss or a special touch before you clip them into their car seat or stroller
- Do a walking meditation while you head to your destination

Aim for one outing a day, or each week, depending on your comfort level. It's even better if you plan to go somewhere with other people who have babies too. It's good for you and your little one to connect with people who are in the same stage as you. You can find groups like this though your hospital, birthing center, or doula agency. Or through the local library or a music or yoga studio. Ask around when you are at the park. Remember most people are looking to connect too. Don't be afraid to strike up a conversation. You may make a new friend for you and your baby.

Assess

When you return home, take a moment to reflect on your outing while it's still fresh in your mind. Did you have the supplies you needed? Restock your bag for next time. Were there items you brought that you didn't need? Remove them to avoid carrying too much. Then add a small ritual to mark the end of your adventure, such as:

- Doing one self-care activity, like taking a drink of water or a deep breath
- Doing a quick gratitude practice to reflect on the good things that happened
- Using energy work to quickly release anything you may have picked up along the way

Remember, getting out and about with your baby can be beneficial for both of you. Don't let worries hold you back. Allow your mindful practices to help you be present and you'll begin savor your "getting out and about" ritual, looking forward to it as part of your day.

Time for You

Caring for a new baby can be all-consuming, leaving you feeling drained and lost in the process. Remember to be kind to yourself and practice self-compassion (learn more in chapter 1) by including yourself in the practice of rituals. Looking for little ways to sprinkle a mindful ritual into your day nurtures *your* mind, body, and soul. Start small, with one thing each day, such as:

- Doing a meditation in the shower
- Lighting a candle or incense when you wake up in the morning
- Writing your hope for the day in a journal
- Doing a quick stretch or yoga pose to release tension
- Saying a daily affirmation or mantra
- Simply sitting in silence, focusing on your breath, and being still

Try to really be present for your one thing, your ritual. How often are you in the shower thinking of your to-do list, worrying about something that might happen or fretting about something that already did?

Give your attention to what you're doing, just washing your body. The more you can bring in rituals with elements of stillness, observation, and intention, the more you'll fill yourself up, from inside out.

Your Partner and You Time

It's hard to remember how you filled your days before children came. Suddenly every second is so full of baby! Prioritizing some time for just you is hard enough, but if you have a partner, making time for you *and* your partner is easy to overlook.

Creating rituals with your partner can help carve out time for you to tend to each other and your relationship. Children learn so much by what they see and feel from their parents, by what you model. In the same way that your physical space can impact your child (read more about that in chapter 7), the space between you and your partner also needs to be Nurtured. You have to take care of each other and that third entity that is your relationship—make a ritual of Nurturing your relationship.

Communicate, communicate, communicate

Keeping up communication helps to keep your partnership strong. As it is often advised to newly married couples, "Communicate obsessively!" And while that might seem excessive, it really is helpful when it comes to family flow. This way you can talk about what you're feeling and what you need. When you hold it all in, you aren't processing and whatever is unspoken can build up walls between you. Make communication into a daily ritual. Work together to find ways, however brief, to create a ritual of open and regular communication.

- *Daily mantra*: Create a shared mantra for the day, such as "Today, we will support each other's goals."
- *Morning connection*: Add in some mindfulness to the morning gameplan. Share your goals and gratitudes over a cup of coffee.
- *Lunchtime check-in*: Send a text or make a quick call to connect and share your day's progress.
- *Evening reflection*: Before you fall asleep, hold hands, share something good that happened, and set intentions for the next day.

Quality time together

Making a little time, weaving a moment here and a moment there, can make a big difference to your overall well-being. It's about quality, not quantity—as quantity is limited with all the attention a "little one" takes. If there is anyone outside of your family who can offer childcare support, be diligent about setting up a time for them to care for your baby and use that time to be with your partner and do something together that you enjoyed before the baby came. It will become a ritual for your caretaker too! It may take some time to feel comfortable with a caretaker. Here are some ways to add ritual when you only have a few moments:

- Share a smile and a moment of gratitude as the sun sets.
- Take a short break to hug each other, releasing stress and reconnecting.
- Take a few deep breaths together, synchronizing your breath and calming your minds.
- Do a quick stretch together (bring baby along!), loosening up and energizing your bodies.
- Choose a touch (perhaps a squeeze or tap) that tells your partner, *I'm thinking of you*, as you pass them.

Watch your words

As an expansion on the Words chapter, watch your words with your partner too. We can sometimes be hardest on the ones we love most. Our loved ones see us at our best and our worst. Be intentional to choose words that raise your partner up, especially when they are having a hard time. Create a reset ritual so you remember to pause, breathe, and recenter when only negative thoughts are swirling. Here are some intentional ways to watch your words:

- Share three things you appreciate about each other once a week.
- Select a word that embodies what you want more of in your relationship, like joy or connection, and find ways to sprinkle it into conversation.
- Whisper a quick "thank you" when you walk by.
- Chant a mantra or sing a song together with your baby at bedtime.
- Hug. Sometimes actions speak louder than words.

Your well of compassion, empathy, and understanding may be pretty empty by the end of the day, but that's exactly why rituals are important for recentering yourself. The more you create supportive rituals, the more you will find yourself able to support yourself and your partner.

Last but Not Least . . .

Long after your little one's hand is too big to fit into yours, you'll cherish the sweet rituals you shared, like morning walks, bedtime baths, and afternoon outdoor play. And you'll see the rituals evolve as your children grow. Embrace the journey, and trust that the Nurture Method's principles of stillness, observation, and intention will guide you in creating Nurturing rituals for you and your family to enjoy.

11

Sleep

OVERVIEW

The Nurture Method and Sleep

Stillness: Be the stillness your little one needs and offer a calm and reassuring presence that helps them feel secure and comforted, making it easier for them to drift off to sleep.

Observation: Observe your baby's sleepy cues, noticing the subtle changes in their behavior, body language, and energy, allowing you to respond with sensitivity and care.

Intention: Approach sleep with an intention not to make them sleep but to create a peaceful environment that nurtures their well-being and trust.

Oh, sleep. There are so many difficult moments in child-rearing, but sleep comes with its own very unique set of challenges. When your baby isn't sleeping, you aren't sleeping. And when you aren't sleeping, well, there are physical, emotional, and mental repercussions. In the trials and tribulations of sleep (or lack thereof), Nurturing practices that help you stay connected, grounded, and loving are desperately needed. There are a myriad of sleep strategies and hundreds, perhaps thousands, of books written on the subject, but we've selected and adapted practices that most align with the Nurture Method.

HOW IT WORKS

Your peacefully sleeping baby is a sight you'll never tire of. Even as they grow, seeing them curled up and away in dreamland allows you to momentarily forget how frustrated, sleep deprived, or overwhelmed you may be. It's a taste of bliss that gives you the strength to do it all again the next day.

Parents learn to appreciate sleep-full nights because they become all too familiar with sleep-less nights. Early on, your little ones are learning so many new skills, and so are you. They have to learn sleep skills too, including how to fall asleep, settle, self-soothe, and re-settle. At first, you do it for them, soothing, rocking, hushing, feeding. There's no other way.

Learning a New Skill

But just as they have to learn the skills to move, eat, and talk on their own, they eventually have to learn the skills to sleep on their own. There is no one-size-fits-all for teaching them how to soothe, settle, and fall asleep. That is why you'll find countless books, methods, and strategies out there. But there are a few practices that you can adopt as you go about the process of teaching them to sleep and finding the method that works best for your child.

The Gift of Sleep

Giving your child the tools and setting up an atmosphere for them to sleep well is a gift. They will get sick, have wild imaginative dreams, and move through developmental leaps and bounds that take them away from their sleep as they grow and grow. Having a strong base helps them move through these sleep disruptions so everyone returns to healthy nights of sleep—and that is a gift to your whole family.

In just the first four months, you can observe significant changes in your baby's sleep patterns. Newborn babies are very sleepy and can be passed from person to person and sleep through it all. Though newborns sleep a lot, their sleep is light and restless as they go in and out of deep sleep. This makes sense because babies' stomachs are still small so they don't take in as much food at a time and need to wake about every two hours to feed. Gradually, they take in more food and can extend their sleep time.

At around two weeks, babies become a little less sleepy and they begin to require more soothing to help them fall and stay asleep. You can't over-soothe or spoil your baby during these first few months. Generally, newborn fussiness tends to start at around two to three weeks, peak at six weeks, and eases up by three to four months when their sleep cycle changes considerably.

Sleep Regressions, Progressions, Leaps, and Wakings

Starting at four months, babies progress to be developmentally capable of falling asleep on their own and self-settling and soothing themselves back to sleep, whereas in the first few months you need to do it for them through rocking, swaying, feeding, walking, or simply holding them close. *Rest assured, even the most colicky babies' fussiness usually eases around the four-month mark due to this developmental leap.* Changes in sleep patterns are often due to new stages and leaps in their development and while it is commonly referred to as a "regression," it is indeed a "progression." This is why teaching your baby to self-soothe and re-settle becomes important for the first time around four months, which is when their sleep cycle changes to the two-hour sleep cycle that adults have.

Teaching them to self-settle—by putting them down to sleep when they are drowsy and not fully asleep and giving them a moment to see if they can re-settle and soothe themselves back to sleep when they wake up—will help them learn to go back to sleep on their own when they wake (after their new two-hour cycle) instead of you doing it for them. Beyond four months, the rocking and bouncing doesn't work as it once did when they were newborns. It takes much longer and becomes more tiresome and harder for parents to settle them. So, it's an optimal time to set that foundation that will help them through all their progressions that are to come.

More on this will be covered in the techniques section, but know that you're not alone in that feeling of frustration over sleep changes. Just when you think you've established a good routine, developmental changes can come along and set you back to square one, forcing you to return to the foundational elements and reset. Their brains are literally waking them to practice their new skills at night. This is "neuroplasticity" in action, our brain's ability to rewire and form new neural connections throughout life to adapt to new experiences. Thankfully, this is happening in adults' brains too, maybe not as rapidly and readily, but we too are wired to adapt and change to changes in our environment. It's exactly what we need with babies, especially when it comes to sleep!

Mindfulness Practices and Sleep

We know that mindfulness is linked to well-being through enhanced emotional regulation and stress management, but how does it relate to sleep? Although research on mindfulness and baby sleep is still developing, existing studies suggest that mindfulness practices in both adults and children can lead to improved behavior and sleep. As noted in the *Journal of Child and Family Studies*, "mindfulness-based parenting interventions have been shown to significantly improve both parenting practices and child behavior outcomes, highlighting their potential as effective tools for enhancing family dynamics."[1] Many studies show better behavior, including improved sleep, in children when parents practice mindfulness techniques at home. As your baby is learning how to sleep better, integrating your mindfulness practices can help you manage the stress of sleepless nights. You will be better equipped to handle those really tough moments because you'll have a practice to keep you present and grounded, proactive instead of reactive. You will be able to catch your autopilot filling in the gaps, telling you that it will never end, and you'll know that this is only a moment in time that will pass. You'll have words, songs, mantras, breathing, stories, energy work, and more to support you. And with those tools, you will be able to bring the calming energy your baby needs to find their way to sweet, sweet sleep.

And with practice, both you and your baby will enjoy better sleep, leading to greater harmony at home. After all, who doesn't benefit from a good night's sleep? And if the data supports mindfulness practices helping with that, sign us up!

TECHNIQUES

The techniques we lay out here are broken into two sections: zero to four months and four+ months.

The separation of technique is because during your baby's first few months, they need you to soothe, settle, re-settle them to sleep. They are not capable of doing it on their own. After four months, they become able to sleep for longer stretches and learn the skills to self-soothe, fall asleep, and stay asleep on their own. There are always exceptions, so we always encourage you to check with your doctor on specific situations, but these are general guidelines that you can start with as you develop your own plan.

Zero to Four Months

The first few months of a baby's life are often referred to as the fourth trimester. It is a very overwhelming time for your baby as they get used to life outside the womb. Inside the womb, they were cradled, hearing a constant hum of noises, held in a space that was the perfect temperature, with food coming exactly as needed, just the right amount of movement, and soothed by the thump-thump of a steady heartbeat. They felt totally safe and comfortable. Then, rather abruptly, everything changes, and they are literally thrust into a world of new and different sounds, scents, and sensations. This is why many babies take until around twelve weeks to find their groove and become more content, and it's also why soothing techniques are needed during these first months.

Slow down

The first few months with your newborn are such a special time that is often looked back upon as a blur. It is so hands-on, so all-encompassing physically, mentally, and emotionally. You are doing so much for your baby, and that takes so much out of you. Amid all of the new experiences and challenges with learning to care for your baby are moments of pure sweetness and joy.

It's a time period unlike anything else. You can never be fully prepared for the extreme highs and lows you will experience until you are in it. Having the tools to stay calm goes a long way toward making it through this time while staying Nurtured and being present for all the moments of joy.

Allow the Nurture Method and the tools we share to help you through this time, and create your own rhythm and ritual.

As you find your own rhythm, keep in mind that babies do cry. Sometimes they just need to cry as they work through so many new and different feelings and sensations at the same time as their internal systems are maturing. Remember *that discomfort can be part of the process* and that we all have different tolerances for discomfort, as evidenced by different temperaments that you see in babies. Tapping into your own intuition is your greatest tool for figuring out why your baby is crying or what they might need. It will guide you along and has the answers for how to best meet the needs of your little one. Mindfulness can help you to turn off your inner chatter and tune into your inner guidance instead. Oftentimes there is no perfect answer or linear or logical next step. You just have to go with what feels right. Pivot and try again.

You'll also want to accept the help of others during this time. There is no extra credit for doing it all on your own. There is a reason why they say, "It takes a village"—because it does, and our current family situations are not set up to allow us to support one another as they once were. Reach out to family, say yes to offers for help, tap into community resources, and remember to allow you and your partner to care for one another as you also care for your baby.

Soothing

Many sleep experts have written about ways to soothe your baby. Here are the few that we feel are most Nurturing:

Skin-to-Skin Contact: At the hospital, you'll hear the nurses recommending skin-to-skin contact, but you don't need to reserve it just for your time in the hospital. Remember skin-to-skin touch when you are at home, when your baby is having a hard time or even anytime that you want to give them extra comfort and connection. Take off their top and yours, lay them on your chest, put a blanket over both or you, and see how it calms them. This isn't an activity reserved for moms, any trusted person can connect and support baby through skin-to-skin contact.

Swaddling: Swaddling imitates the continuous touch and snug cuddling of the womb. This helps babies feel safe and helps control their startle reflex. When you think of how your baby was held so tightly inside the womb, you can see why swaddling can be so soothing. Swaddling for nap and bedtime is a practice to continue as part of your routine for the first few months, until your baby starts rolling over. At that time, you want to stop swaddling and look into sleep sacks so the baby can safely roll around. At the hospital is a great time to practice your swaddling, with the nurses there to assist and demonstrate the different methods of swaddling. Like anything, the more you do it, the easier it becomes. Beyond using a blanket, there are different types of swaddles you can buy or get secondhand. Swaddling may become an important part of your soothing repertoire.

Side/Stomach Position: Babies find being on their side or stomach to be very soothing, as well. This works only when you are holding your baby or watching them closely and is not for sleep (as you know, the back is always best for sleep). This is why babies love being held and worn so much, because when they are, they are often on their stomach or side, right near your heart (see position diagrams in the holding section below). This position can also be incredibly soothing for a baby who is feeling discomfort or gas. The pressure on their tummy helps to relieve the discomfort they are feeling. Coupling the side position with shush and pat will also be a strategy for teaching them to self-soothe when they are a little older (more detail on this in the four+ month section that follows) but it's great to plant the seed now. It leads to the next soothing technique, the shushing sound.

Sound: The sound of white noise or your own shushing is another way to soothe your baby. It imitates the loud sounds of the womb that your baby is used to hearing. Having a white noise machine in your baby's sleep space helps to set up a soothing environment for your baby. You can even have a portable one that you move along with the baby as they sleep in different spots. Also, your own strong hushing (such as making a CHHH or SHHH sound) right near their ear can be very soothing. Anytime you are holding and rocking, the *Shhh* sound or singing a lullaby is very calming for your baby. They love the sound of your voice along with that shushing noise. This is a great moment to use mindful breathing, mantra, singing, or words and sprinkle in a little extra Nurturing.

Swinging: Whenever someone holds a baby, you often see them naturally move into that rhythmic back and forth motion—the sway. That rocking, swinging movement soothes babies because it's like the movement they felt in the womb, and we tend to do it naturally as we hold babies because it works. It is why wearing your baby in a sling, pushing your baby in a stroller, or even driving them in a car can help them to calm. Having a swing or bouncer for your baby helps them to get that movement when you can't do it yourself. When you are not sure what else to do, get moving, swinging, marching or even dancing with your baby, and see how it helps them calm.

Sucking: Sucking on your nipple, clean finger, or pacifier is another way to help your baby soothe. You'll only want to use a pacifier once breastfeeding/bottle feeding is established as you don't want to create confusion for a baby who is still learning to eat. Once feeding is finished, consider your clean finger or a pacifier to help them settle and soothe. If one type of pacifier doesn't seem to work, you can try a different one.

Hold: Holding your baby in a different position may be just what they need. Here are a couple of ideas for different ways to hold your baby that could help them feel greater comfort and ease.

1. Football Hold.
    This works especially well for a fussy baby with gas or colic. Cradle your baby's head in your hand, supporting their neck with their face turned outward and your forearm supporting the rest of their body. You can link your two hands together for added support. You can't see a baby's face too well when they're in this position, but it's a good position when you think stomach discomfort or gas may be the issue. The pressure on their tummy can help.

Football Hold.

2. Reverse Breastfeeding Hold.
    This works well when you are bouncing them into calm. It's easy, comfortable, and perfectly supports their head and neck. Swaddle your baby first. After they are in the swaddle, you hold your baby horizontally facing outward.

Sleep 135

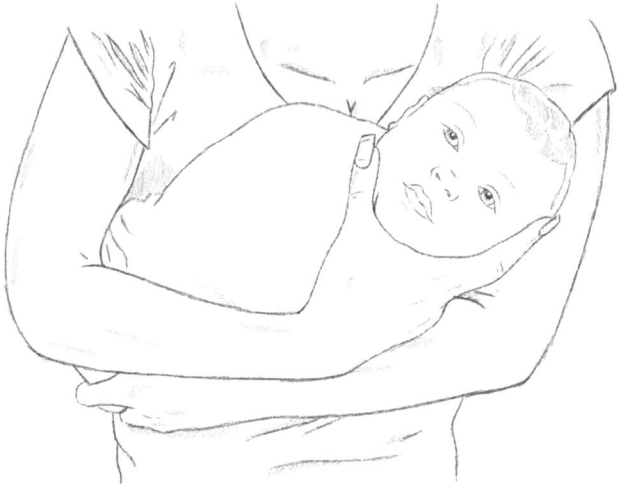

Reverse Breastfeeding Hold.

3. Over the Shoulder Hold.
   Lifting your baby to an upright position with their head above or around your shoulder, supported by your hand, can often have a strong, soothing effect. They love the feeling of their fussy tummy against your upper chest and shoulder. It's like tummy time on you. Also, you are close to the baby's face, and they love that. It's also a helpful position for keeping the baby asleep as you transfer them to the bassinet or crib.

Over the Shoulder Hold.

4. Gentle Touch on Baby's Chest.
   Placing your hands on baby's chest when they are lying down is soothing for the baby. When you lay them down, you can place your hand on their chest, maybe say a little affirmation or "Sleep well, *name*," or "I love you" or add some energy work. This can also be a helpful strategy when you are doing sleep training and want to soothe the baby and let them know you're here but not pick them up.

Gentle Touch on Baby's Chest technique.

5. Wear Your Baby.
   Most babies feel very at ease when they are being worn. The closeness to you and movement are very calming. It also gives you a chance to be hands-free for a little bit. You can use this time to go on an Adventure, in your home or around the area (a walk in nature can be calming for you and baby) or you could do some deep breathing which will help you relax and can put your baby right to sleep.

Wear Your Baby technique.

6. Take a Break.

    You can always lay the baby on their back in a safe space like their bassinet and take a break if you need to. A little space will help you and your baby, as they may just be overstimulated. By taking a pause, you will help yourself recenter and return to your baby with greater calm and a renewed ability to tune into your baby.

Four+ Months

Most babies make great developmental strides around the four-month mark. They become more responsive at this time, they cry less, smile more, have more consistent patterns, can do some self-settling, and therefore are able to resettle themselves and sleep for longer stretches. This is a time when you can begin to follow a more rhythmic pattern with two or three consistently timed naps during the day and longer stretches of sleep at night.

All of these practices are available to you before four months, but recognize your baby will not be developmentally ready to adopt them. Once they cross that three-month mark, you can begin to teach them to begin to soothe, settle, and sleep on their own.

Consistency

Having a sleep ritual can be one of the best practices toward creating positive sleep for your baby. Your sleep ritual comprises the environment you create and the pattern you follow right before sleep time. This set of consistent activities creates a flow that helps babies to recognize it is sleep time and naturally wind down. It looks a little different for everyone, but below are a few elements you could include in your ritual. You will also find more information on bedtime rituals in chapter 10.

- *Light.*
  We all have a circadian rhythm, and you'll see this beginning to develop in your baby as early as six weeks. While at first your baby does not understand nights or days, light is one way to help their inner clock naturally develop. This means moving toward starting the day around 7:00 a.m. and winding down around 7:00 p.m. Working with the natural cycle of light helps them to develop their own rhythm and have it sync with real time, which will create better flow for your family. You'll want to create a nighttime feel at nap times with low light (shades closed) and limited stimulation and create a livelier feel at their awake times with lots of sunlight (shades open) and extra activity.
- *Naps and Nighttime.*
  As you learned in "Rituals" (chapter 10), evening bedtime is a natural time to establish your sleep ritual. Making sure your baby is not overtired is key. You'll begin to see that having a consistent sleep ritual will help your baby with their naps during the day. And good sleep during the day leads to longer stretches at night. In the early months, many babies nap while being held or on the go in a stroller or their car seat. By four months, you'll want to move toward them napping in a dedicated space that is the same place as where they sleep at night. This will be a good time to start following a sleep ritual. Babies love consistency and predictability, so having a ritual helps with their sleep.

- *Environment.*
    Creating a calm and consistent sleep environment is another important component for teaching your baby to fall asleep on their own. Calming colors, music, white noise, appropriate light, and a special space all help your baby to not get overstimulated and be better able to fall asleep. You can read more about creating a Nurturing environment in chapter 7. Where your baby sleeps depends on what works best for you and your family. The American Association of Pediatrics recommends infants share a parents' room, but not a bed, "ideally for a year, but at least for six months" to reduce the risk of sudden infant death syndrome (SIDS). Wherever works best for your family is best, and staying consistent and allowing the baby to fall asleep in the same place they wake up helps them re-settle on their own instead of needing to be held, fed, or rocked back to sleep.
- *Bath.*
    Many babies find a bath to be very comforting and soothing, and it might be a good addition to your nighttime routine. The AAP recommends bathing your infant three times a week until their first birthday. Beyond the age of one, when your baby grows to a toddler and begins eating, crawling, walking, and getting into much more, nightly baths may be necessary, so it's a nice practice to start now.
- *Cuddle, Books, Massage, and Song.*
    Once your baby is in their space and calm, it is a great time to have some bonding time, such as cuddling and deep breathing (chapter 6), reading a book (chapter 9), massage, energy work (chapter 12), singing a song (chapter 4), or saying a prayer or mantra (chapter 5). Many people find saying the exact same words right before bed can be really effective such as "Good Night, Baby. Sleep well. I love you. See you in the morning." You want to do what feels good for you and your baby, and your ritual will soon become a very special time for both of you.

If there is something your baby does not seem to jive with yet, like maybe a bath, you probably don't want to make that part of your routine. Do it in the morning when you and your baby feel fresher. Stress for you or your baby does not help sleep. And keep in mind, you'll want to do a shortened version of this nighttime ritual for naps to maintain the consistency and help them establish consistent naps. It can be harder for your baby to settle down and sleep at naptime than it is at night, because of sunlight, more activity. However, keeping up the consistency of flow and ritual, your baby will nap, and it will only help their mood and ability to sleep better at night.

Self-Soothing

After three months, many babies become capable of doing some soothing and settling themselves. One of the tricks to teaching your baby to self-soothe (meaning they are able to soothe themselves back to sleep after one of their sleep cycles and thus stay asleep longer) is to put your baby down to sleep when they are drowsy but awake.

Babies under three months often need to be rocked, bounced, and soothed to sleep and then are able to be placed in their bassinet and stay asleep during the transfer. As babies get older, they are more likely to wake up when you transfer them from your chest to the bassinet. Instead, you prepare them for sleep, and once they are drowsy, put them down.

Start by putting your baby down still awake for one nap a day, and gradually move toward doing this for all of their sleeps. The first morning nap of the day tends to be the easiest for babies to fall asleep, so start with that one. If they have already fallen asleep, you can consider tickling their chin or touching their cheek, to rouse them slightly so they open their eyes before you place them down to sleep.

For night and nap wakings, try to comfort and reassure your baby by patting and soothing with your voice and gentle touch before picking them up and taking them out of bed. As your baby lies in the crib, whisper, "Shh, shh, shh," while patting their back and holding them on their side. If they can't settle in the crib, try picking them up and in a similar way gently pat or rub the center of their back with a steady rhythmic motion and put your mouth to their ear and whisper, "Shh . . . shh . . . shh." As soon as they stop crying, gently lay them back down.

Give them a moment to work it out or use your voice or gentle touch to settle them over picking them up right away.

This is teaching your baby to soothe themselves, to find resilience and answers within themselves. It also helps if they fall asleep in the same place that they'll wake from a sleep cycle rather than falling asleep in your arms. Falling asleep in their beds helps them to re-settle back to sleep on their own.

If the shush and pat isn't enough to calm them, you can continue to pick them up when they cry then put them back down once they stop. You don't hold them until they are completely calm and almost asleep. Only until the crying stops. This is sometimes called the Pick Up/Put Down method. You pick them up, then put them back down once they stop crying.

You are offering comfort while they put themselves back to sleep (instead of you doing it for them). You want your presence to be felt and your voice to be heard. This will help comfort the baby and teach her to soothe herself back to sleep knowing you are there with her as she practices this new skill. Being consistent with your routine and your responses creates positive sleep habits for them.

Be mindful . . . of sleep cues

Being observant of your baby's sleep cues is helpful for getting your baby back to sleep before they get overtired. It is true that sleep begets sleep. The more they sleep, the happier and less overtired they are.

Remember to be aware of your baby's awake time (which is the time between when they wake up and go back down to sleep). As a newborn, their optimal awake time is only 30–60 minutes, which is just enough time for a change, a feed, couple minutes of alert time, then right back to sleep.

Babies' awake window gradually increases as they get older and become a little more aware and alert. By twelve to sixteen weeks, you can expect their awake time to be around 90–120 minutes. At this time, they may have their days and nights figured out and will be sleeping longer stretches at night.

Their awake window at night is much shorter, and you want them to be back to sleep right after their feed with little stimulation/activity.

A good rule of thumb for the daytime is to make sure your baby always goes back to sleep within around two hours of waking up during their first year. Meaning they wake up, have a full feeding, have some stimulation/play, and then should be back down to sleep two hours later.

You know to begin your bedtime routine once you see sleep cues such as these:

- Reduced activity, seeming bored
- Yawning, jerking arms
- Staring, blinking, and rubbing the eyes
- Red appearance on eyebrows or under eyes

Take these ideas in stride. Trust us, you will find your flow. All families do. Beyond all of these ideas and strategies, following the Nurture Method principles of being still, observing, and being intentional will be your greatest tool as you teach your baby to self-soothe and sleep well on their own. There is never a better time than now to start. The older babies get, the harder it gets to break old habits and create new positive ones. But wherever you are is the perfect place to get started. Give yourself some grace and meet yourself and your baby right where you are. Sleep can be exceptionally challenging to find anything Nurturing in—but don't give up. Look at part 3, where we lay out NEST (Nourish, Energize, Sleep, Tend), which is a consistent pattern that you can cycle through each day to create the flow and consistency that you desire and that will support you in getting the sleep you and your baby need.

12

Energy

OVERVIEW

Energy Work and the Nurture Method

Stillness: Connect with your baby's energetic body by becoming still and allowing the sensations to become noticeable.

Observation: Observe what the energy feels like in all your senses, note how it changes as you move, pay attention to what your intuition is telling you.

Intention: Bring your focus to the energy body, set your intention to provide whatever your baby's energetic body needs.

Energy healing works with the body's electrical system and vibrational frequencies to reduce pain, improve well-being, and regulate the nervous system. When you can tap into mindful connection with your baby's energetic body, you will see how simple, loving touch can be a powerful tool for your baby's health and happiness.

HOW IT WORKS

There are a lot of things that we know that work, like gravity, but we're not exactly sure why. Energy healing is one of those things. Modern science has just started to explore the practice, and what they've discovered so far is that for some reason, it works.

Recent studies[1] have shown that energy healing can help reduce physical and emotional pain, improve the outcomes of surgery, decrease the side effects of chemotherapy, and regulate the nervous system—just to name a few benefits. Not too shabby, right?

Why? No one is entirely sure yet. But here's what we do know:

We know that the body is an electrical system. We know that at the subatomic level, matter is vibration. We know that being touched is essential to humans. We know that belief in healing is a big part of the healing process.

And we know energy medicine incorporates all of these things. So it stands to reason that the practice would be helpful to people.

So whatever the reason, the benefits are too big to ignore at this point, and U.S. hospitals are starting to incorporate energy healing into their treatments. The American Nurses Credentialing Center, the world's largest and most prestigious nurse credentialing organization, includes an energy healing modality (Healing Touch) in its continuing education programming.

While modern medicine is slowly getting on board with energy healing, our ancestors have been in on the secret for thousands of years. Energy medicine has been a part of almost every culture throughout the millennia. It has different names and different forms but it's the same concept: our body extends beyond what we can see with the naked eye, and this energy needs TLC just like the rest of us.

Training

If energy healing is so powerful, should it be practiced without any formal training? Acupuncture? No. Please do not try to stick needles into your child. But hands-on energy healing? Yes. The reason is the same reason you don't need a license to give your partner a massage when they come home with a stiff neck. We all have an innate ability to care for each other that does not require logging hours under supervision. The basic mechanics of the energy medicine taught here is about simple connection and loving touch. The techniques are there as a guide to help you learn to work within the energy body, but as you become more adept at listening to the subtle sensations of energy, you will probably find yourself going "off script" as you move where the energy is instead of where this book tells you to go.

Spirituality

Energy medicine and spirituality often go hand-in-hand, but they are not inexorably intertwined. You do not need a faith and you are not ascribing to any faith when you use energy medicine. In many ways energy work is as spiritual as flying in an airplane. You can look out the window of the plane and see nothing is holding you up, but know that the mechanics of the universe are, in fact, working perfectly and that you are being held up by the laws of physics.

In the same way, just because you can't see the energy body that you're working on doesn't mean it's not there. It only means you can't see the electrical system of the body or the vibrations of the subatomic structure of matter with your naked eye.

As with anything in your life, your faith can become a component. You are always welcome to bring your faith to whatever you're doing, but that is a supplement to the practice, not a requirement.

TECHNIQUES

Try It on Yourself

If you're new to the concept of energy healing or think that only certain people can do it, then start with this simple exercise.

Place your hands twelve inches apart from each other and then, very slowly, bring them together, paying close attention to any sensations you feel. You might feel something right away or it might not be until your hands are a centimeter apart. You might feel something warm or cold, prickly, tingling, buzzing, thick, sticky, rough, or smooth. It's usually very subtle, so subtle that you don't notice it unless you're really paying attention. We'll talk more about what "it" is later on.

For now—if you do feel something, stop and explore the sensation for a moment. How would you describe it? Does it change when you move your hands around? Move a little closer and see if the sensation shifts or gets stronger.

Not feeling anything? That's ok. It may take time. Or you may not feel anything at all. Just because you're not picking up on a sensation doesn't mean you're not sharing the benefits of energy work.

Some people also report that they see colors or hear noises instead of feeling energy (this is a neurological condition called synesthesia, in which one sense is simultaneously perceived by one or more additional senses. Did you know that some people taste colors and hear numbers?), so just notice if maybe an image or sound comes to mind as you try this.

The most important thing to remember is that there's no "right way." Much like parenting, each experience is unique, and we have to do what works for us and our babies.

Putting It into Action

Simply put: the goal of energy work is to smooth out the kinks in our energy field and get that energy moving again. Think of it, again, like a massage. Only instead of working with muscles that may be a little out of whack and causing some discomfort, you are working with the body's electrical field that may be a little out of whack and causing some discomfort.

We will introduce you to some energy work techniques that we have developed based on various energy work practices and adapted to what we have found to work best with small children. But as you read through these techniques, remember that there's a common saying in the practice, "intention over form." Your child will get the most benefit out of you doing what feels right rather than by following a set of steps.

As you practice energy work, let your little one inspire you. Become like a child. They don't ask the hows and whys. They are only present in the moment, and if something works, it works! So let them be your guide and simply go with the flow, letting the energy direct you. If something feels bumpy, smooth it out. If it feels spiky, pull it out! If something feels like it needs concentrated touch, hold your hand there. Your rational adult mind may ask questions and cast doubts ("Am I really feeling anything?" "How is this actually helping?") but if those things come up, just set them aside for later.

At the end of this chapter, we will go over some suggested sessions for you to try but ultimately, you should create a session based on what you observe as you begin the practice.

Contraindications

Energy work has not been found to have any adverse effects. And it does not in any way interfere with conventional medical care. However, because the calming nature of energy work can induce a lower heart rate, we do not recommend these procedures for a child who is medically sedated or on heavy painkillers such as morphine or fentanyl.

Setup

By now, you may have noticed a theme when it comes to energy work: go with the flow! If you go to an energy work session as an adult, you'll likely be in a dark, quiet room, lying on a massage table with calm music playing. But obviously it's not so simple with babies. So, you're going to have to go with the flow. A lot of the time, it won't work to plan to do energy work on babies ahead of time—if there's a moment, seize it!

Here are some suggestions for your setup:

- Location: You need a space where you can easily reach your baby from head to toe with both your hands. Changing tables and playmats make perfect spots for doing a little energy work. Bassinets and cribs tend to be problematic because they are too low, too high, or have a railing you have to reach over.
- Setting: If you can, lower the shades or turn down the lights. Put on some calming music. This is also a great opportunity to use mantras (chapter 5) and your breath (chapter 6) to help you stay focused.
- Mood:

If they're awake and wiggly, make it a joyful and fun experience! Smile and be present with them. Tell them what you're doing. "Wow! I feel something bumpy here with your tummy, let's get that smoothed out!"

If they're sleeping, perfect! What a great time to perform energy healing. It's not uncommon for adults to fall asleep during an energy work session, and it's when some of the best healing can take place. Make this a meditative practice and enjoy this quiet time with your little one.

If they're crabby, proceed as you see best. Energy work can help with pain and discomfort, so it may be exactly what they need. But they also might need to be held or fed or played with or put to bed. Bring your calmest, gentlest self to the practice, and if it's just not working, don't force it.

Note: Feel free to bring in a toy or lovie to help them keep still. They don't need to be focused on you to get the benefits.

Steps

IMPORTANT NOTE BEFORE PROCEEDING: We covered this at the beginning of the book, but since this tool is called "healing" and "medicine" it bears extra repetition here. Energy work is not a substitute for consulting with a physician. It should also be used only as a complement to conventional medicine, never as a replacement. While energy work has been known to have healing properties, these statements have not been evaluated by regulatory authorities. It is always best to discuss any alternative therapies with a medical doctor first.

1. **Opening**
   Tune Up
   - Always begin each session by getting yourself ready first. Think of it as putting on your own oxygen mask before helping others. It's never a good idea to try and perform energy work if you're not feeling calm and centered. So, take a moment to get there.
   - Close your eyes (if your baby is somewhere they can roll off of, keep your hand on them!).
   - Take in a deep breath. Then another.
   - Notice if you are holding any tension in your body and give it permission to let go.
   - Now, literally, get *grounded*. Imagine yourself taking root into the earth. Picture your legs like the trunk of a tree and feel your roots reaching down into the ground. Roots are an incredible system that deliver nutrients from the soil—so go with that imagery. See yourself connected firmly to the earth, receiving everything you need.
   - Once you feel strong and rooted, you can open yourself up to the energy world. With your eyes still closed, become aware of all the movement and vibrations around you. The sound of your baby cooing is a form of energy moving around you. The light seeping in past your eyelids is a form of energy. Is there a fan moving the air? Is the carpet tickling your feet? What sensations are you picking up on? Can you start to home in on those sensations and pay attention to them in a way you normally don't when you are hurrying about your day?

- When you feel connected to the energy world, set an intention to have a practice that is supportive to your child. You might say to yourself, "I am here to listen to my child and offer what they need at this moment." If you have a spiritual belief, now is a good time to invite your higher power to join you. This can all be done in ten to fifteen seconds, though if you can take longer and it feels good, do it!

Tune In with Your Baby

Tune In technique.

- Now that you are all tuned up, it's time to get in tune with your baby! Take hold of their precious feet with each hand. You can hold their whole foot with your hand or place your thumb on the bottom of each foot. Look at your beautiful little one and smile. Appreciate this moment you have to connect with them.
- Share with them the intention you just made. You can share it silently or if they're awake, maybe say it out loud. "Okay sweet pea! You ready? Let's do some energy work together. You show me what you need, okay? I'll listen and support you."

2. Energy Techniques

You will always do an opening and closing but would typically not do all of these procedures in a single session. Instead, you will have them in your toolbox and let the energy and your intuition inform you as to the right steps. At the end of this chapter, we'll share some ways you might use some of these techniques in different situations.

Technique #1: Energy checkup
An energy checkup is a great way to start. This is an easy way to get a general sense of what's going on and find any particular areas you might want to pay extra attention to.

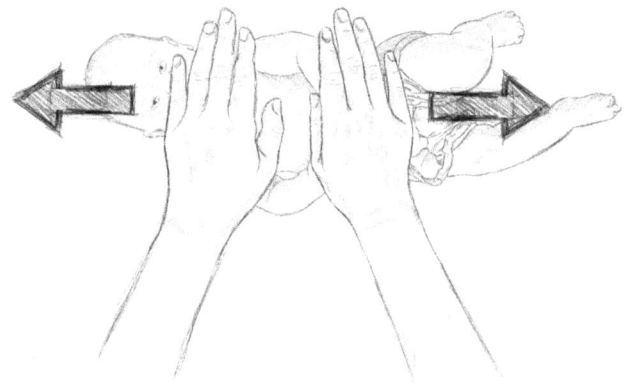

Energy Checkup technique.

- Place your hands side by side, several inches above your baby's stomach. Very slowly, separate your hands—move one hand towards their head and the other toward their feet.
- Take note of any sensations along the way. Is there a warm spot over their throat? A bumpy patch over their tummy? What else are you picking up on?

Once you've done your check in, you can decide what you would like to do next.

Technique #2: Peaceful Pass
This is a basic procedure for smoothing out any disruptions in the energy field.

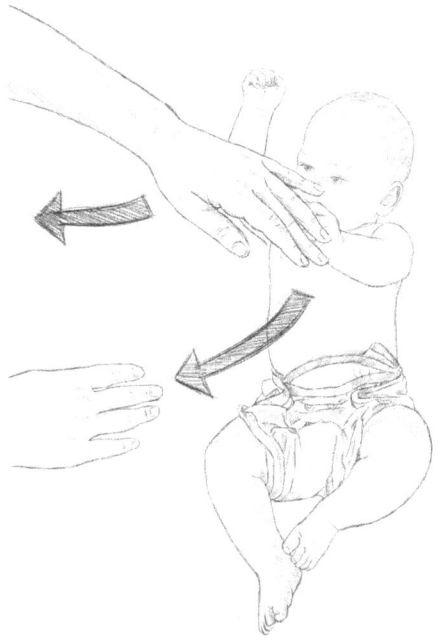

Peaceful Pass technique.

- Starting at the crown, place your hands a few inches above your child's body and brush them down each side of their body, like you are sweeping dirt off a counter. Swish, swish, swish your hands—fast enough to get energy moving but not so fast that you can't feel sensations along the way. Go straight down the middle, then on the left, then on the right, around ten times each or as many as it takes until things start to feel smooth.
- Spend extra time on any spots you noticed during the checkup and wait until the energy dissipates. If it does not, try a different technique.

Chapter 12

Technique #3: Loving Hold
If you felt a singular area of energy, perhaps a cold spot or a small circle of sensation, or if you know there is an area of physical discomfort for your child, this simple action can provide much relief.

- Place your hands directly onto your child either on the spot where you feel the energy sensations or on the area where they may have some pain, such as a tooth coming in. You may notice the sensation becomes stronger when you do this.
- Breathe in and out and simply wait for the sensation to dissipate. You might tell your baby, "Uh-oh, something is stuck here! Let's help it get moving."

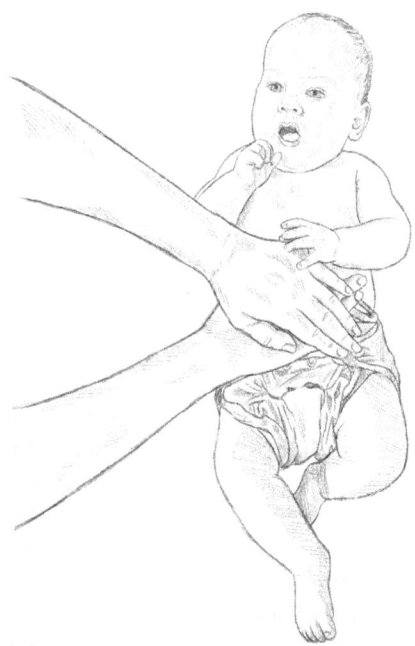

Loving Hold technique.

Technique #4: Petals of Release
Sometimes energy can feel like it is blossoming outward, almost like a flower. This kind of disruption is easily released by pulling the energy up and out.

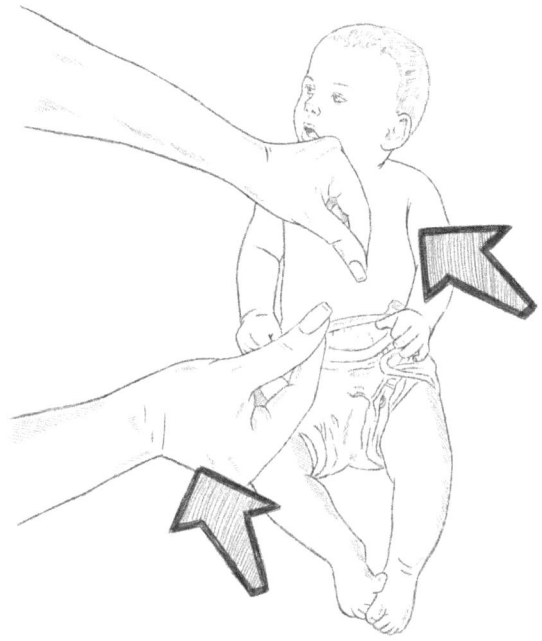

Petals of Release technique.

- Locate where the energy rises up and use your hands and fingers to grasp it.
- Pluck it by very gently lifting upward, as if you were plucking a petal from a flower.
- At the end of your pull, fling the energy away the same way you might fling a petal to the ground. Like the petal going back into the earth, you are sending the energy back into the earth.
- Repeat this with both hands until you feel the sensation reduce or go away.

Technique #5: Energy Swaddle
Energy might poke up, feeling as big and dramatic as a baby meltdown. That's when it's time to swaddle the disruption with some gentle care.

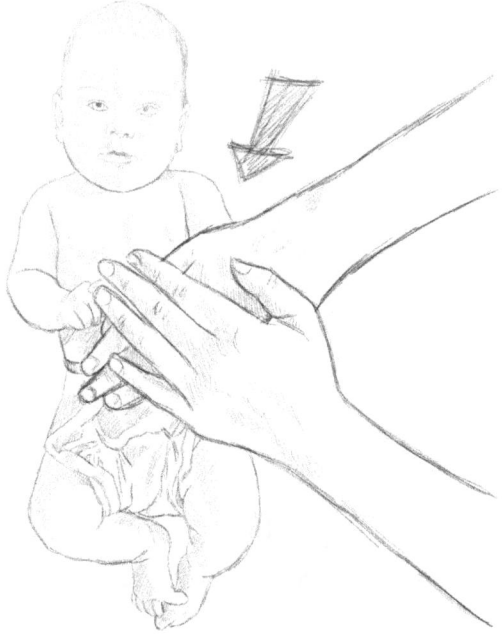

Energy Swaddle technique.

- Locate the top of the energy disruption.
- Placing your hands on top of each other, then slowly lower them toward your baby.
- When your hands reach your baby, hold them on your baby, with the same firmness as a swaddle might hold them.
- Wait for a few seconds and then repeat, noting how the sensation changes or goes away.

Technique #6: Body Harmony
This sweet and fun technique can support the rapid growth taking place inside your child and to help them connect to their body as a whole.

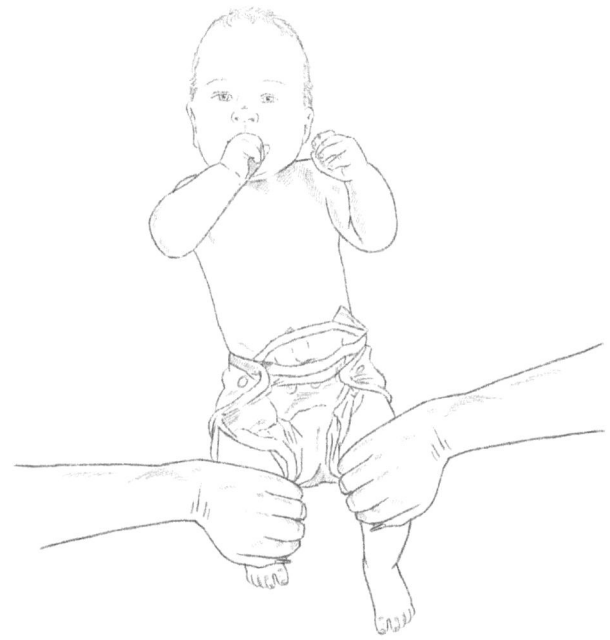

Body Harmony technique.

- For this technique, you will put light pressure on their body. Do not squeeze any parts of the body, but instead gently hold your hands on each spot.
- Try to keep your hands on each spot for at least five seconds. If you feel a sensation or simply the desire, hold your hands in a spot for longer. It can be helpful to envision a warm healing light coming from your hands and enveloping the area of the body you're touching.

- This is a fun, extended version of "head, shoulders, knees, and toes" so if your baby is engaged, talk them through what you're doing! Name each part of the body and tell them what you're feeling.
  1. Begin by placing both of your hands on their head. Hold at least five seconds, but the longer the better.
  2. From here, begin to work your way down, moving one hand over the other, "connecting" each part. Here is our suggested order:
     a. Place your right hand on the baby's head (crown) and your left hand above their brow (space between the eyebrows).
     b. Now, place your left hand on their brow as you move your right hand to their throat. Cup your right hand gently around the throat, with your palm facing the baby, and avoid applying pressure.
     c. Place both hands on their heart.
     d. Keep your right hand on their heart and move your left hand to their right shoulder.
     e. Place your right hand on the left shoulder.
     f. Move your hands down, placing your left hand on their right elbow and your right hand on their left elbow.
     g. Place your left hand on their right hand and your right hand on their left hand.
     h. Place both hands above the baby's stomach, with your left hand on the right side and your right hand on the left side.
     i. Keeping your right hand on their stomach, move your left hand to their right hip.
     j. Place your right hand on their left hip.
     k. Move your hands down, placing your left hand on their right knee and your right hand on their left knee.
     l. Finally, place your left hand on their right foot and your right hand on their left foot.
  3. With your hands on their feet, hold and take a deep breath. Then slide your hands off their feet, as if you are pulling little socks off. Allow the energy you moved and connected to move freely.

Technique #7: Slow Soothe
This is a wonderful practice to do at the end of the day or any time you want to bring some calming energy to your baby.

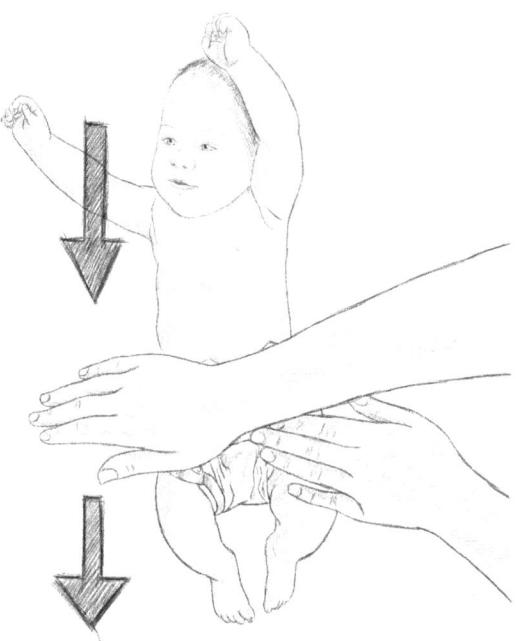

Slow Soothe technique.

- With one or two hands a few inches above your child's body, start at their head and pass your hands over their body like you are smoothing the wrinkles out of a sheet.
- Repeat this ten times or many times as you would like!
- This movement can be done fairly easily with one hand and is wonderful for when you are rocking them to sleep, feeding them, or even playing on the play mat.

Technique #8: Tummy Release
Want to get things moving? This is an excellent way to help unstick stuck intestines. Bonus: it works really well on grown-up intestines too!

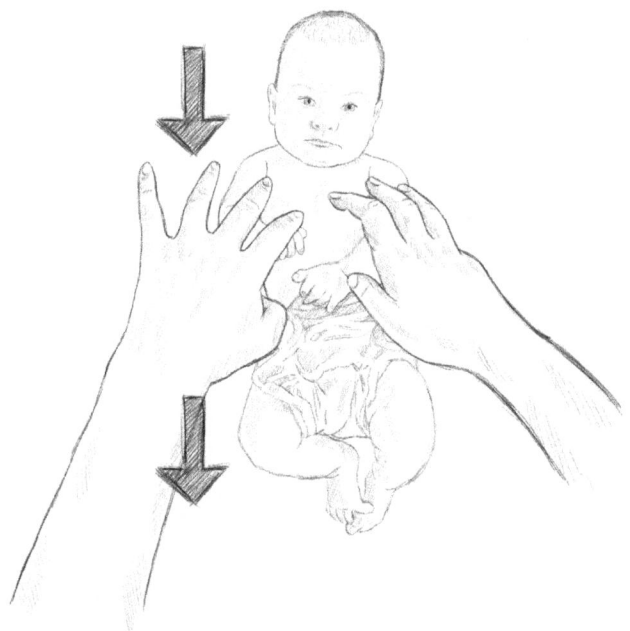

Tummy Release technique.

- Place your hands next to each other, a few inches above your baby, and spread your fingers wide. Point your fingers toward your baby and "rake" your hands from the top of their body, toward the bottom.
- Repeat this ten to twenty times. The more times you can do this, the better. Then just stand back and wait for the reckoning!

Energy 159

3. **Closing and Grounding**
   At the end of every session, finish by releasing your connection.

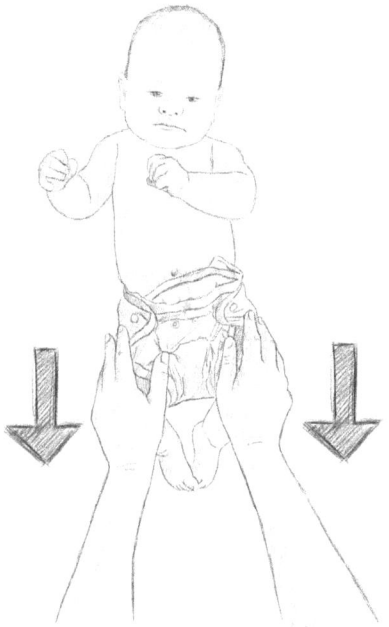

Closing and Grounding technique.

- Place your hands on your baby's legs and quickly brush your hands down past their feet three times. This will help release any energy that may still be lingering from the work you did and will also help release any energy that may have been transferred to you.
- End the way you began, take hold of their head and take a deep breath. As you breathe in, it's nice to indulge in a moment of gratitude for this time with your child and for the ability to connect with them in this special way.
- As you breathe out, release their head.

Sample Sessions

Here are just a few ways you can use these procedures. You'll always want to start by getting tuned in, connecting with your baby, and then doing an overall energy assessment. When you're done, do a final energy assessment to see how things feel, and then ground and release.

During Playtime

Energy work can be such a fun time together! When baby is lying on the floor, use your hands and your touch to entertain them. Mind-body connection is a fantastic way to help them learn about their bodies while they receive the benefit of energy work. Here is one possible sequence you can try:

Tune Up
Tune In
Checkup
Body Harmony
Checkup
Closing and Grounding

After Getting Their Shots at the Doctor's Office

Poor little one. In addition to some Motrin, energy work can help relieve pain and provide relief after getting a shot. The Peaceful Pass will help move everything through the body quicker, and the focused healing can be used at the injection site to soothe any pain or soreness. Here's a sample sequence that you can try:

Tune Up
Tune In
Evaluation
Peaceful Pass
Energy Swaddle
Evaluation
Closing and Grounding

Preparing for Bed

Energy work is ideal for a bedtime ritual because it is so calming! Right after that pre-sleepy time diaper change, keep them on the changing table and use energy work to help prepare them for sleep. The Loving Hold can be used to smooth their energy and allow their body to heal and grow better overnight, but you can easily switch that out for whatever you think they need, like a Tummy Release.

Tune Up
Tune In
Evaluation
Slow Soothe
Loving Hold
Evaluation
Closing and Grounding

These are just a few very short sessions that can be done in a few minutes. But there's no time limit on energy work. You can put every energy technique on the menu or spend an hour just doing the Body Harmony.

Here are a few other ideas for when you might use these techniques:

While they are sleeping: Watching your perfect baby sleep in their bassinet? Use the time to share a little healing with them.
Before a procedure: Medical procedures and hospital visits might be a reality for you. Use energy work as a way to prepare your little one's body and to help them feel connected to you even when you are separated
Car seat catastrophe: Stuck in the car with a screaming baby? Pull over or, if someone else is driving, move into the back seat and use your hands to help them feel more comfortable.
Sibling love: Invite any siblings to be part of the process. They can either receive healing from you (you can use one hand on each child or switch between children) or help you perform energy work with the baby!

PART 3

INTEGRATING THE NURTURE METHOD

13

Okay, Now What

Wow, that was a lot.

So . . . now what?

At this point, you might find yourself thinking, "Okay, got it! Implement these steps, and *mindfulness for me and my baby achieved*!"

Or you might find yourself thinking, "Oh my gosh, this is *too much*. I can't possibly accomplish all this!"

Well, we've got some good news and some bad news.

The good news is that you don't have to accomplish it all!

That's because the Nurture Method and mindfulness are skills. And, like any other skill, you have to work at it. You can't wake up one day, decide you want to start running and then run a marathon. You need to practice (practice, practice!). The same goes for mindfulness. It's not like one day you will wake up and "be mindful." It's a skill that you must practice and keep working at. And it's an important one. Just as your body needs food, rest, and exercise, your mind and soul needs stillness, observation, and intention to stay well.

The bad news (although, is it really bad?) is that you can't *achieve* mindfulness either. Just like you can't run a marathon and stay in shape, mindfulness is an *ongoing* practice. A beloved yoga teacher used to say, "If you can perfect a yoga pose, then throw it away and never do it again, because it has nothing left to offer you." Think about it: if you are strong enough and flexible enough to do a *perfect* yoga pose, then what is your body getting out of it other than showing off to the rest of us in the room? The same goes for just about anything in your life. If you can run without breaking a sweat, are you even exercising? If you are in a perfect state of mindfulness 24/7, do you even have children screaming in your ear and creating beautiful baby chaos? The journey is the destination, so enjoy the process, the sweating, the stretching, because that's when you are getting all the yummy stuff out of the work.

Luckily, we don't need to be marathon runners to exercise (thank goodness). And we don't need to be Zen masters to be mindful. Wherever you are in your practice is exactly where you need to be and is the perfect place to start.

So now that you know that this is going to be a lifelong project, here are some ways you can start to integrate the Nurture Method using mindfulness as your guide.

REDEFINE GOOD AND BAD

As you begin to integrate these concepts and techniques into your everyday, there's something very important you need to do: let go of that all-too-familiar voice that defines things as "good" or "bad."

Did you ever hear the Taoist story of the farmer? It goes a little something like this:

One day a farmer's horse ran away. When his neighbors heard the news, they came over right away.

"OMG, bad luck," they said.

"Maybe," the farmer replied.

The next morning the horse returned and brought another wild horse along with it.

"Wow that's great!" the neighbors told him.

"Maybe," replied the farmer.

The next day, his son tried to ride the wild horse, was thrown, and broke his leg.

The neighbors were back, offering their condolences. "That's too bad!"

"Maybe," said the farmer.

The following day, military officials came to the village to draft the young men into the army, but because his son's leg was broken, they left him.

The neighbors congratulated the farmer.

And the farmer said (you got it . . .), "Maybe."

Be the farmer as you explore and integrate the Nurture Method into your day-to-day. Let what works "well" or "makes sense" or seems "weird" or "didn't go great" instead just "be." When the "neighbors" show up in your mind and start telling you what's good or bad, just smile and say to them, "Maybe."

Prioritize What's Most Important

Our culture has picked up on the whole idea of keeping our physical bodies well. You can't go too long without hearing about what to eat or how to move your body to keep it fit. We know to "Just Do It" and "no pain, no gain." We know we have to eat our greens and gulp down our vitamins. Even if we don't always do it, we know we should. And we know there will be discomfort that we need to push through to get to the benefits.

But the messages about the need for mindfulness, the need for presence, the need to be still, to take time in the quiet to keep your mind and soul well, those messages don't come across so much. And it is a need. When you bring mindfulness into your life, it impacts every corner of your life. You sleep better, feel better, grow better, breathe better, learn better—you just live *better*.

So, as you begin your practice, put mindfulness in the same category as you do healthy eating and exercise. Make it a priority for yourself and your family. And know that no pain, no gain. Not that mindfulness hurts, promise! But it might make you uncomfortable. Your mindfulness practice will call you to connect with yourself and what is happening around you. This may not always feel comfortable, especially at first. You may be reluctant or afraid to take away the distractions and be present in the moment. That's okay—it's totally normal. Anything new can be scary and hard. But if you're not stepping out and leaning into things that are hard or uncomfortable, you're not growing, and that's no way to live.

But with pain (well, discomfort), comes gain! As you begin making time to implement your practice, you will feel the positive reverberations inside yourself and your home. The effect is subtle and cumulative. You may not feel the benefit in the moment, but later in the day, or the week, or the month, you will begin to feel it. That's because your practices are creating a different level of awareness within you. As you become more aware, you recognize when you are in an agitated, frustrated, or other low-energy state. As you become aware, you make a shift, and don't stay in that place.

Start Small

Being home with a new baby is a natural time to create new habits. You are probably home more now. While your days are fuller, as you care for your baby around the clock, you may feel a slowdown as well. A slowdown that many parents with older children look back upon longingly.

It's best to embrace the slowdown by indeed slowing down. Yet, use the time to also integrate some new meaningful practices that will last well beyond this stage and become ingrained in your family flow.

We've shared a lot of techniques, but we discourage you from trying to do it all. Instead, start small by integrating one that stands out to you. Make that one a big priority so it becomes a part of your world and your family's ritual (learn how to implement rituals in chapter 10). When that new practice is in place, then consider adding another one. You want to allow the momentum of actually integrating that first new practice to propel you into trying something else.

Don't Wait till Tomorrow

How many times have you allowed the thought that you are already too far behind to start something new? Now is the perfect time.

Too often we let the promise of tomorrow deter us from fully experiencing and making the most out of today. This is the essence of mindfulness in many ways. Be here now.

If that isn't enough motivation, the research supports the vital importance of putting energy into creating a Nurturing family home environment. "The family environment is one of the most essential contributors to and predictors of children's subjective well-being and life satisfaction. A good family environment is characterized by mutuality, stability and closeness as well as parental care, warmth and emotional support."[1] So the question is, *if not now, then when*? You want to take steps forward now that are going to make tomorrow better for you and your family.

You Do You

Your Nurture Method is unique for you and your family. No two Nurture Methods will be exactly the same. Do what feels good for you. Don't try to do the things that work best for your mom friends or best friends or your parents. It's good to get advice, but in the end, you need to tune into yourself, to trust your own voice. There is no child on this planet that is exactly like yours. And there is no person on the planet that is exactly like you. So you have to trust your own self when it comes to doing what's right for you and your baby. You are the expert on your baby.

The more you do this mindfulness work, the easier it becomes to listen to and trust that voice within you. You are creating space to be able to hear and trust that voice. Taking action becomes easier the more you do it. You have to take that first step. It's always the hardest—and especially hard if you look outside of yourself for what that first step should be. It comes from within, and you'll know it's your truth because you will feel how right it is for you.

Be Kind to Yourself

Feelings of guilt, shame, and comparison become too close of companions for too many new parents. It's really easy to compare yourself to others who seem to have it all figured out. Let us remind you, nobody has it figured out when it comes to being a parent. They may look perfect and seamless as you scroll through parenting videos on TikTok. Remember that is their highlight reel. When we compare ourselves to others, those comparisons are our neighbors stopping by to judge, and we may be left with feelings of inferiority or superiority—and neither creates well-being and joy.

You have all you need inside you to give your baby all that they needs. You have to be present in order to tune into your guiding voice. You also have to know you will make mistakes, but stay compassionate with yourself. Affirm that you did the best you could, and trust that it's all part of the process and was something you needed to learn.

Remember to be kind to yourself with your practice and with your parenting. It's not always easy to be kind to yourself. But know that as you are, you model self-compassion and kindness for your little one. As you practice being kind, accepting, and patient with yourself and your partner, your baby learns to be that way too. (Check out the Self-Compassion meditation in chapter 1.)

All the techniques we share are here to help you create your own practice to keep you centered. When you are centered, you will still experience ups and downs, but you will move through them with more ease, returning more quickly to your own rhythm.

Expect Only Reality

The Nurture Method is not here to help you live like a Pinterest page with unattainable presentations of photoshopped fantasies. *Nailed It* memes need not apply to your mindfulness practice. Do not—we repeat—do not try to do everything in this book, and do not try to do any of it "perfectly."

This book is about *everyday* mindfulness with children. Being mindful will look a little different for you *every day*, because each day brings with it its own challenges and opportunities. You will end some days feeling like it was the worst day of your life (we actually cover that in chapter 15). This is life. This is especially life with small humans. There are many unknowns and unexpecteds when a new human enters your life, and that leads to much uncertainty. And uncertainty is not easy as a parent or otherwise.

If you have a baby, only one thing is certain: most of your days will be full of poop, tears (yours and theirs), and too few winks of sleep. And that's on top of whatever else you may have going on—other children, aging parents, physical health issues, mental health struggles, financial struggles, a dog that isn't taking the new addition well and is chewing up the house, you name it.

When things don't go as you expect, as they often won't, you may feel like a failure. Too often we equate failing at one thing as failing at everything, and it's hard to find our way out from that cloudy perspective. Remember, if your day feels like a fail (and no amount of mindfulness practices can prevent those days), *you* are not a failure. You tried. You did the best you could. Your baby loves you, even when you feel like nothing is going right. It can be alluring to stay in that place of gloom. The Nurture Method helps you catch yourself in that dreary, self-loathing place and, with greater awareness and compassion for yourself, you can make a shift. Nurturing yourself is as important as Nurturing your baby. What's amazing about being a parent is that you have a living, breathing, beautiful reason right in front of you, this little helpless being who only has eyes for you, to help you get out of that funk. The Nurture Method helps you focus more on what's going right—there is always at least one thing—and less on what's going wrong. Each new moment is a chance to start fresh and, by practicing the techniques, you will do just that, and teach your little one to do it too.

So set your expectations to the poopy, tearful, sleepless reality that is life with a baby and know it doesn't last forever. Making it look seamless and picture perfect all the time is not the goal, because it's not reality. The goal is to treat mindfulness like a spice, and to sprinkle in the Nurture Method—not dump the whole jar in at once. The more you sprinkle these practices into your daily life, the more you will see that there is so much love in the messiness of every day, because it is authentic, real, and true. So allow yourself to just be, do less, and take it one day, one moment at a time. You may not be able to see yourself getting through the whole day, but you can get through this moment. This moment right now is all your baby is thinking about, and they don't care about Pinterest pretty, they just want real, authentic, and a little bit messy you.

For Ages Zero to Ninety-Nine

This book was written with parents of babies in mind, but the Nurture Method, its application and techniques, will work for parents with children of any age. What you learn can be adapted to benefit your children at any age, even if your children are having children of their own (and beyond!). Just like your child will progress from milk to soft foods to finger foods to begging you to order pizza, so your child will grow in their practice of mindfulness. Their tastes, desires, and abilities become more complex with age, yet the fundamental need for Nurturing in body and mind remains. You don't stop giving your children bananas simply because they don't need soft foods anymore. In the same way, you don't stop modeling mindful practices like supportive rituals, healing energy work, or Nurturing words, when they get words of their own. You simply look for new ways to nurture and feed them exactly what their growing bodies and minds need.

When the time comes, and it will come quickly, that you feel they have outgrown a technique, don't just put it away. Instead, look at how you can adapt it and update your recipe to meet your new needs based on the core principles of the Nurture Method—accepting your child wholly as their own authentic being; staying present amid what is coming up in life; trusting that what is coming up, even if it's hard, is what life is all about. Remember that by going through it together, you create a special connection, keep growing, and find meaning in your life.

The more you follow the principles of the Nurture Method and practice the techniques, the more centered you'll stay amid the many ups and downs, transitions, and stages that come with being a parent. Your modeling of these mindfulness practices and adapting the different techniques based on what comes up in your family life helps your children learn these techniques and build a strong foundation that will stay with them and help mindfulness to take root in them so they can grow into their best selves. Wherever you or your children are now is the perfect place to start. Every little bit of the Nurture Method makes an impact, however and whenever you can sprinkle it in.

It Takes a Village

It takes a village to raise a child. Creating consistency and predictability for your child from home to the grandparents' house to the child-care center, the better off your child is. A child with deep roots and a strong foundation stays grounded even amid the natural challenges life brings. We know that the vast majority of critical brain development happens in the first five years of life. It's time we equip the village with the Nurture Method so it can give children the tools to build the solid foundation that will help them grow into their highest and best. Share this book, or your favorite tools, with your village, with anyone who has regular interaction with child. The village is stronger when more of its children, our future, experience positive, productive growth and development, especially in the critical first five years of their lives.

14

Nurture in Action
NEST

NEST is an acronym for the components that will help you create a healthy family life: Nourish, Energize, Sleep, and Tend.

We created NEST, a practical methodology and set of techniques to sprinkle into your day to help you and your children (through your modeling) to be more mindful and present. By NESTing, you prepare yourself and your environment in a way that lets babies receive what they need most: your presence, your attention, and your love—so they feel seen, heard, and know that they matter just as they are.

NEST encompasses being mindful and creating a space (or nest) that is comforting, calming, and predictable (babies thrive on predictability).

Many women begin "nesting" in pregnancy. They feel the desire to clean, organize, and prepare their home for the arrival of a new baby, but nesting isn't only for mothers, and it doesn't stop when the baby is born. We feel it's important that everyone caring for a child to continue to prepare your nest so that you feel comfortable and at peace in your space well after your baby arrives.

CREATING YOUR OWN NEST

It's not always easy to think about establishing a rhythm in the chaos of family life, when it feels like every moment is just about trying to get through the day.

But as your family gets used to having this new little being around, you may find that some patterns begin to emerge. And from those patterns, you can create routines that work for all of you. And then, within your routine, you can integrate your mindfulness practices. As you read more, you'll see that you can make your mindfulness practices part of many different activities throughout your day, not just in the quiet moments.

NEST is a flexible framework designed to help you establish a rhythm that works for you and your baby. It's not a rigid structure, but rather a guiding principle to create consistency and predictability in your daily routine. By following NEST, you'll create a sense of security and familiarity for your baby, who thrives on knowing what comes next.

Remember, NEST is not set in stone; it's a dynamic guide that adapts to your baby's changing needs as they grow. The basic pattern remains the core foundation, but the specifics will evolve over time. As your baby develops and matures, you'll naturally adjust the rhythm to accommodate their new needs, interests, and abilities.

As you navigate the journey of parenthood, NEST, like the Nurture Method, will remain a trusted companion, helping you create a rhythm that harmonizes with your baby's ever-changing needs.

NEST EXPLAINED

1. *Nourish.*

Nourish is the first element in NEST because it's an integral part of the rhythm of your day and your baby's healthy growth and development.

Nourish is a reminder to nourish yourself as much as you nourish your baby.

Some days it may feel like you are doing nothing but nourishing your baby. But you have to remember to nourish yourself too. It's easy to overlook your own needs as a new parent. Look to your partner or your community to help you, whether that be grocery shopping for you, helping you prepare balanced foods that fill you up in a good way, and sharing feeding times so you have a chance to eat too. Have healthy snacks handy for when you need something quick. This is a time to try and let go of guilt and shame around food and fill your body up as best you can, giving yourself grace when it is needed.

This can be a mindfulness practice as you try to be very present with whatever food you are eating as it nourishes your body and gives you energy.

2. *Energize.*

There will be certain activities throughout your day that give you energy and other ones that take that energy away. The Energize element reminds you to weave in some time to cultivate the energy you need for the moment and what's coming next. You can read to your child, sing to them, or take them on adventures. Use this time with *intention* to make the most of baby's energy and awake time as they grow into rolling, crawling, walking, playing.

This is also time to look for things that will bring you Nurturing energy; incorporate them into your activities with your little one.

For instance, if they enjoy lying on the floor and watching a mobile, you can use that time to lie next to them and do some restorative yoga stretches. And of course, a walk outside in nature can be especially life-giving!

Adjust this time as needed, but making it a part of your flow will help you and baby feel better physically, which will help you stay clear and connect with your heart, mind, and soul.

3. *Sleep.*

We know how essential sleep is for your baby. It's when they grow, and having a positive sleep routine is good for your baby's development and temperament. Contrary to some widely held beliefs, sleep begets sleep. Good naps during the day make for longer stretches at night, because one needs to be relaxed to sleep well. When your baby sleeps, so can you. Work together with your partner, a postpartum doula if that is an option for you, or any other helper you have to make sure everyone is getting as much rest as possible.

Creating a routine around sleep that you use during the day at nap times as well as at night creates consistency and positive associations for your baby and helps everyone stay rested.

4. *Tend.*

Last is tend. We've talked about what it is that your baby needs more than anything—it's your attention. Tending to your baby is the most loving thing you can do. It's just as important to tend to yourself.

Notice what you need to feel good and tend to it to make it happen. If baby is asleep, use this time to do something that fills you up. Maybe it's sleep, maybe it's a shower or walk or sitting down to a meal. Carving time for you into your routine helps ensure you aren't overlooked.

Caring for yourself is often the first thing you let slide, but it's essential to your well-being.

Also, remember to care for your partner or loved ones and to keep your other relationships healthy and well-tended.

Why NEST?

Following this NEST pattern throughout your day helps you create a rhythm and be in flow. If you don't have a rhythm, each day could be completely different and unpredictable. This can be very hard on you and your baby. But just like ritual, it doesn't need to be *exactly the same* each day, but the guiding principles will allow you to create consistency.

When creating a rhythm, it also helps to develop positive practices that you will remember and cherish long after your baby graduates from them. When you are in a good flow, you will find a way to naturally give attention to the things that matter most.

As we discussed, what you focus on grows and will lead to you creating more moments of meaning and joy when you are focusing on the right things. The moments of challenges and frustration will still be there, but having a rhythm and some tools to help you get recentered when you get off course matters. It matters because showing up as your highest self, with your love and attention, is the greatest gift you can give to your baby.

Babies' rapidly growing brains form neural pathways based on what they feel in their environment and what the person they love most—you—model in your own interactions and responses.

Following a rhythm like NEST throughout your day will help you to stress less, appreciate more, and create a more consistent and calmer atmosphere that babies and toddlers thrive in.
NEST helps you find your flow and be more present so you can savor the fleeting time with your little one that is indeed the longest and shortest.

Reality Check

In chapter 13, we encouraged you to accept reality, and it's important that we stop here to review that again. The reality of life with a baby is that you need to reset expectations and recenter often. Things do go wrong, you will be uncomfortable, and there will be uncertainty.

Below we offer some examples of how to integrate NEST into your day. While we try to show that it can be used in all kinds of situations, at the end of the day, it's important to remember that none of these sample days are your reality. We can't possibly account for all the things that life will throw at you in a day or how you will somehow manage to juggle all those things while sleep-deprived. Don't read these as samples of what should be or what could be. It isn't and they aren't. Like all of the Nurture Method, approach these by asking yourself, "What sounds good? What feels good? What can I take from this and sprinkle into my own life?"

Sample NEST Day 1: Creating a Daily Schedule around NEST

The NEST method at its fullest can be a complete schedule for you and your newborn. Each aspect of NEST, used throughout the day, can follow your baby's normal rhythms in a healthy and supportive way. Here, we show how it can be implemented during the busy day of a stay-at-home parent with an older child and baby.

Nourish
7:00 a.m. Baby wakes! Before you drag your tired self out of bed, you set an *intention* for the day to see if you can find small ways to be present with your family during the day.
7:30 a.m. During the first nursing/bottle feeding of the day, you do some *ujayi breathing* to help bring some nourishing oxygen to both of

you. Big brother is bouncing in and out of the room and you invite him to join you in the breathing exercises whenever he makes an appearance.

Energize
8:00 a.m. It's going to be a busy day of running errands and taking big brother to activities, but you've got ten minutes for some *mindful playing* to energize you and your baby. You and big brother explore the nursery, having him point at different patterns and objects around the room and explain them to the baby.

Sleep
9:00 a.m. Baby goes down for a nap.

Tend
9:15 a.m. You race to get a quick shower, setting up your toddler with some Daniel Tiger on the PBS kids app (a nice learning show that he adores). And, instead of playing music, you use the five minutes (if you're lucky!) to be *in the stillness*. This way you can hear if baby wakes or big brother is getting into anything he shouldn't. You spend the rest of the time doing one-on-one time, singing and playing with your toddler until baby wakes.

Nourish
10:00 a.m. Snack time! You head to your *mindful space*, and while baby nurses, you and big brother munch on some pre-cut fruit and veggies (you asked your mom to do that for you while she was over on Sunday) which made it much easier to grab with baby nursing.

Energize
10:30 a.m. And you're off! Baby and brother are loaded in the car and you're starting your day. On the way, you play some *mantra* music and sing along.

Sleep
1:00 p.m. You're parked outside, waiting for big brother to finish his activity, and the baby is napping in the back seat.

Tend
1:10 p.m. In addition to catching up on e-mails and phone calls while big brother is in class and your baby is sleeping, you *meditate* for five minutes.

Nourish
2:00 p.m. Baby wakes up and it's time for another feeding. You practice *self-care* by hydrating.

Energize
2:30 p.m. Back home and the three of you are playing together. You have big brother help you with some *creative storytelling*, maybe a story about those noisy neighbors from the Taoist tale in chapter 13 of this book, who love to judge what's good and bad? Observe how this creative play energizes your toddler to do some imaginative play on his own.

Sleep
4:00 p.m. You take big brother and baby for a walk in the stroller so baby gets in a short late afternoon nap and big brother gets some quiet time.

Tend
4:30 p.m. You use your walk to be present. You notice the tension you've been holding in your body (no surprise, it's been a busy day) and you *relax into the moment*, letting go of the hustle and bustle that's behind you.

Nourish
5:00 p.m. Dinner time for the kids. While they eat, you use your *words* to appreciate what happened during the day.

Energize
6:30 p.m. While your partner bathes big brother, you get the baby ready for bed. While baby is on the changing table, you spend a few minutes doing some *calming energy work* to help them, and you, relax.

Sleep
7:00 p.m. As you put baby down to bed, you sing them a *special song*, to the tune of "Twinkle, Twinkle Little Star," that talks about everything they did and saw and learned during the day. It's a part of your wind-down routine that you do with your toddler, too, that helps both of them ease into bed.

Tend
7:30 p.m. PHEW! You did it! Both kiddos are in bed. You and your partner have dinner and a part of you wants to stay up and hang and then do your gratitude practice, but actually you're just too tired, and it's going to be an early night. You congratulate yourself on having *compassion* and doing what you and your body need.

Sample NEST Day 2: Embracing Life with a Newborn

NEST is more than a schedule; it can also serve as the four pillars that uplift you throughout your day.

You may not like the regimen of a schedule, your life may not allow for one, or the schedule you had may all fall to pieces (more on that in the next chapter). No matter what your life brings, you can practice NEST as a way to incorporate the Nurture Method and stay more grounded. In this way, you can enjoy the many joyful moments while moving through the overwhelming moments with greater calm and grace.

Nourish
7:00 a.m. The sun is rising outside your window as you feed your baby. You take a moment to reflect that the days and nights seem to blur now that you are up and down continuously with feeding every 2–3 hours around the clock. You allow this natural start of the day to be a moment to *mindfully breathe and ground yourself.*

You *affirm* that you are supported, you are strong, and you have everything you need to get through this new day. With this simple practice, this moment of presence, you look at your baby differently.

You feel grateful that you are able to feed and support this little one and are reminded to feed yourself too. You eat one of those bars you leave by your feeding areas along with a big glass of water.

Energize
9:00 a.m. You feel exhausted, and your baby is having trouble soothing back to sleep. It feels like so much effort, but you decide to go for an *adventure* outside with baby to see if she'll sleep in the stroller.

You tell yourself that even if you just make it around the block, it's worth it. You grab your diaper bag that is already packed and ready to go with supplies you'll need, creating a boost of *self-appreciation* that energizes you.

As you look at yourself in the mirror, your inner chatter first goes to your not being put together enough, to the bags under your eyes, and the weight you put on. You pause and choose not to listen to that chatter. You *affirm* that you are strong, you are a great parent, and you are beautiful.

You try to do something that makes you feel like yourself again— today you choose to brush your teeth and put on your favorite hat. *Those two little things make you feel a little energized.* You make it out the door and around that first block and feel better. Your baby has calmed from the fresh air and movement, and you feel energized too. You play with your and baby's senses as you get creative and *create a little story* around everything you both are experiencing during your walk.

Sleep
9:30 a.m. Baby falls asleep, and you decide to walk a little further. You get back home, baby stays asleep in the stroller and you just let them be.

Tend
You know there's dishes in the sink and crumbs on the floor but you know that right now, you need to rest while the baby is resting. You get into bed and do a few deep breaths, just plain deep breaths because you're too tired to remember any techniques, and then you drift off.

Nourish
10:00 a.m. When baby wakes up, you get up and, before feeding baby, you take a much-deserved moment to sit, drink some water, and have a healthy snack.

Energize
11:00 a.m. You are feeling good and so is baby after your morning walk, her morning nap, and a good feed, so you lay them on their mat as you sit next to them and do an extra pump to build up your store of milk. Next, you play some *energizing music* for them and you as you allow them to practice some tummy time. You find it *energizes* you to be ground level next to them as they respond with some adorable little smiles for you.

Sleep
12:00 p.m. Baby goes down for their afternoon nap.

Tend
12:15 p.m. You are able to tend to those house tasks so much more easily than if you hadn't rested. You've set your timer for 30 minutes and challenge yourself to get as much done as you can before it goes off. You've set more realistic standards for yourself and no longer need the place looking immaculate. It's my home, and it's meant to be lived in, you repeat as a *mantra* that calms you.

Nourish
1:30 p.m. You accomplish more than you thought you would and take the last few moments to nurture yourself with a healthy meal, as you know baby will be waking soon. You even do a short *body scan meditation* after eating that leaves you feeling more grounded and calmer for baby's next feed and the late afternoon/evening time that tends to be your baby's fussiest.

Energize
3:00 p.m. You wear baby as you walk around doing your late afternoon tidy-up, a *ritual* where you re-stock your diaper stations and diaper bag, put away things, and set yourself up as best you can. Baby stays content with the movement and as you talk to her about what you are doing as you do it. Baby starts to fuss so you do some *energy work* and massage to help baby soothe into her late-afternoon nap.

Sleep
4:00 p.m. This is baby's fussy time so a nap in her bassinet is often hard. You decide to use your voice to sing a *song* about all that you

did today as you rock them and let them sleep on you. You listen to an audiobook once they're asleep and allow yourself to enjoy this special time of *being still.*

Tend

5:00 p.m. Your partner is home and it feels so good to have another human who talks and walks around, yet all you can think about is taking a shower. You take a breath and a few moments to just be with your partner, a *ritual* you have built in order to be intentional about connecting with each other.

You hug and really feel that embrace and just sink into it. You tell your partner about your biggest high and low from the day. The high, you heard a coo that was the most beautiful sound. The low, a complete blowout all over the changing area and yourself.

You make a mental note to order the next size up in diapers. You take a moment to just be and laugh because you see the humor in how different your days are now than they once were. This moment of connection with your partner actually fills you up, but you know now what you need more than anything is a shower. Your partner wears baby and makes dinner. You hear a bit of chaos in the next room, but you don't let it take away from your shower. You keep your calm and focus by repeating the *mantra* "peace begins with me." With these words, you are reminded that even when life is hard and complicated outside of you, you can find peace within. You play some of your favorite calming *music* and allow yourself to really feel it. You get out of the shower, dress, and feel so much better about doing the next feeding, and that meal your partner made—even though it may not have met your standards a few months ago—tonight you tell them you appreciate them and the meal because you are aware that it is one less thing for you to tend to.

Sample NEST Day 3: In the Hospital

Time has no meaning in a hospital, and none of the doctors and nurses are on a NEST schedule. But you can still bring Nurturing routines into the space. In some instances, you may not be able to even feed your child—but Nurturing is still possible. In this example, we use a breastfeeding parent to show just one way you can still make Nurturing a mindful act under these difficult circumstances.

Nourish

5:20 a.m. The nurse comes by to check on your baby, waking you all from a fitful sleep. You use the opportunity to pump, and as the machine whirs rhythmically, you sing a *mantra* to the beat, inviting peace into your room and into whatever the day may bring.

Energize

11:30 a.m. After a parade of medical staff, it's finally just you and your baby. After a morning of poking and prodding, it's the perfect time for *mindful play* that engages the senses. Use the room, the beeping of the machines, the assortment of tools and supplies, the view out the window, as well as your own healing and comforting touch to help them learn to experience the world outside of their hospital bed.

Sleep

3:50 p.m. More tests in the afternoon. Your baby has slept in fits and spurts throughout the day, but you have been on high alert since the morning. Now, your baby is resting and the room has grown quiet. You want to check your e-mail, pay bills, doomscroll on social media. But in the stillness, you realize that you are tired and should sleep. It doesn't feel like you will ever be able to sleep again, with all the things swirling around in your head. But you lay back and use *4-7-8 breath*, allowing your thoughts to focus on the counting, and you allow the breath to release just enough of the tension in your body so that you are able to drift off.

Tend

8:15 p.m. Your baby is overtired and, frankly, so are you. But at long last, the day is done, and your next nurse visit won't be for another four hours. You turn down the lights and sit down next to your baby's bed to perform *energy work* to help their body calm and heal. You remember all the fancy techniques you learned, but all you can manage is to place your hands on their head and close your eyes, and that's exactly what both of you need.

Sample NEST Day 4: Back to Work

If and when the time comes to return to work, you can still take NEST with you. Being away from your little one doesn't mean that your job as a parent stops while you are away. Using NEST will allow you to connect with yourself and your baby, creating a richer and sweeter bond between the two of you.

Nourish
7:30 a.m. You know you need to rush out the door, you sit down for one last feed with your baby before you go. As you rock them, you engage in some *creative storytelling*. Looking into their eyes, you weave a tale of the great warrior who is going off to bring home supplies for the kingdom and who will battle great challenges (like that big project that's due by noon) to ensure peace in the kingdom.

Energize
12:30 p.m. The midday slump has hit, and all you want to do is go home and snuggle with your baby. It's time for lunch, and today you decide to sit outside. You put your phone away, and instead focus on *engaging your senses*. The taste of the food, the sound of the cars, the feel of the bench on your back. The practice begins to wake up your mind. You have ten minutes left after you eat, so you decide to do some *energy work* by simply placing your hands on your solar plexus, releasing the tension of the day, and welcoming in the healing energy. As you do this, you hold the image of your baby in your mind and share the healing energy with them.

Sleep
7:00 p.m. Home at last and just in time for your baby to go down for the night (sort of). You easily slip into your nighttime *ritual*, something special between you and baby that lets you both release everything from the day and ease into a calm and present place together.

Tend
9:00 p.m. Your sweet angel has already woken a few times, perhaps a signal of what the night holds. They are resting again now, and you find

yourself worrying about just how little sleep you may be getting over the next few hours. As you *observe* your thoughts, you realize the future is unknown and all you can do now is choose your present. You choose self-care. You replace your thoughts of "this will be terrible" with the *mantra* you created, "My love is stronger than my fear." You give yourself permission to go to sleep. And as you close your eyes, you indulge in deep breaths that match the rhythm of your mantra that gently rocks you to sleep, and you know with certainty that whatever awaits you tonight, your love will be strong enough to care for you and your baby.

In Case You Missed It: The key here is to note the "time for you" that is integrated throughout NEST. This is when you can practice mindfulness, you can do some breathing exercises, you can rest. You want to use this time, no matter how short, to fill yourself up with those things that help you to feel like you. It's too easy to lose yourself in the role of parent. That is why having your own practice is important.

15

What to Do When . . .

No time for reading? Need support now? It's okay. *We've got you.*

We've put together a list of some go-to techniques to help with common kiddo challenges. Just flip to that page and start right now.

Before you do, just take a quick breath. You can do this.

What to do when . . .

BABY DOESN'T STOP CRYING

Try *Bumble Bee Breathing* (p. 77). This breathing exercise will not only help calm you, but the funny sound might be just the distraction your little one needs.

Use one of the *soothing holds* (starting on p. 134). Try all of them out and see if there's one that helps them relax a little.

Practice the *Body Harmony energy healing* (p. 155). If you can, integrate that into a full session with an opening, tune up, tune in, energy check up, and then the mind body connection.

Create a more mindful and relaxing space by opening a window and *getting some air* (p. 85). Even if it's chilly or hot out, just a minute or two can help reduce stress and change things up enough to help your child.

No One Is Sleeping

Use the *mantra "Hamsa"* (p. 66) and relax into it. Let your tired mind take a little nap and your nervous system receive some love as you repeat the sounds, "Ham. Sa." I am. I am exhausted but I am strong, I am capable, I am love.

Give yourself and your little one some TLC with a *Slow Soothe energy healing* (p. 157). You might be too tired to do anything more than gently run your hands over your child or you can make it into a quick full session.

When you're sleep deprived, your outlook on your life can quickly take a nosedive. Use your words to help your brain create a more hopeful reality. Even if you don't feel it, choose to speak some *words of appreciation* (p. 45).

In these moments, your rituals will help keep you present. Turn to your *sleep ritual* (p. 119) and let it guide you during this time. If you don't have one, begin creating one.

The Weather Isn't Cooperating

Just because you can't go out doesn't mean you can't go on an adventure. Let stillness, observation, and intention be your sherpas as you go *exploring inside* (p. 108).

Make new plans with your eyes, ears, smell, taste, and touch. *Discover the senses* (p. 94) together with fun and mindful activities.

You are way more entertaining than any other kids' artist out there. Let your creativity flow and *create a song* (p. 58) or two that will be sure to bring some smiles.

Use color (p. 84) to lift your spirits and have a good time while you're at it. Go on a hunt to find every object in the house with a cheerful or calming color.

Routines Change

Routines change but rituals don't, so *find your rhythm* (p. 115) and look for ways to incorporate that into the new routine.

If everyone is feeling out of sorts with the change, use your words to reframe it. Engage in some *creative storytelling* (p. 105). Tell a tale about what's going on that entertains while it helps you and your family put it into a positive light and a more relatable context.

One of the best ways to get grounded is with eye contact. Get in some *facetime* (p. 99) with your child, become present with them, and get in a few giggles.

Feeling overwhelmed? Go *exploring outside* (p. 110) to help reset things. When you come back, start fresh in adjusting to the new routines.

It's Been a Long Day

Your rituals are a lifeline for staying connected. When you're feeling depleted, make sure you don't forget about the *rituals just for you* (p. 122). If you don't have any, choose one and start now.

Find a little nature (p. 111) It might be a walk down the street, some outdoor time in your backyard, or even just playtime by your favorite plant. Find a way to connect with the earth and start reducing stress.

If you can, sit with your child—maybe while you're feeding them, reading to them, or watching TV—and engage in some restorative *ujayi breathing* (p. 75).

Before bed, use the *mantra "pacem"* (p. 66) to bring you and your child back to peace. Shift your focus to peace, invite your body to become peaceful, share the gift of peace with your little one, and envision a peaceful night to come.

It's Been the Worst Day Ever

When these days come, *Choose Love* (p. 49). That's it. On those very worst days when you can't find it in yourself to breathe or sing or practice rituals or try energy healings, that's okay. Take two seconds to choose love: for yourself, for your body, for your child, for your life. That small act, right now, *will* support you and help you take the next step forward.

Epilogue

You know that feeling as the frosty winter begins to thaw and the first buds of spring appear, when you can tell that green leaves and colorful flowers and warm days are just around the corner? There's excitement in the air with the sweet promise that it won't always be cold and dark. Life with littles can be a bit like waiting for spring. Too often we are waiting for the next thing before we can really enjoy it. We wait for the big moments like the next birthday, vacation, season, grade, or milestone to really enjoy it. But our babies are only with us for a short time before they grow up and if we wait for everything to be just right, we may miss the real beauty.

Like winter, life can be cold and dark and so it can be easy to get stuck waiting for the spring. Choosing what's easy over what is important is our natural tendency as humans, but the more you choose what's important over what's easy, the better you feel, the better your life flows, and the more your family benefits.

The Nurture Method is designed to be a springboard to help you to savor all the moments, and it is our sincere intention that the techniques we have shared help you do just that. Because we know that when you Nurture yourself, you will have more access to the patience, love, and joy you need to show up for your baby.

And while we can plant the seeds of mindfulness for our children, in the end, they will make their own choices and live their own lives. The best we can do is give children the deep roots to help them blossom. But in order to do this, we have to blossom first; this happens as we take time in stillness, in observation, and with intention—Nurturing ourselves to grow into who we are supposed to be.

Even though it may be hard, be present for it. This is the greatest season of your life, so make it your own, and make it beautiful.

Notes

PROLOGUE

1. National Scientific Council on the Developing Child. *The science of early childhood development.* Harvard University Press, 2004.
2. Feldman, R., et al. Mindfulness and parental sensitivity: A systematic review. *Journal of Child and Family Studies* 23, no. 10 (2014): 1721–1733.
3. Harnett, P. H., and S. Dawe. The impact of mindfulness on parenting: A systematic review. *Mindfulness* 3, no. 2 (2012): 142–155.
4. Zeidan, F., et al. Mindfulness meditation improves cognition: An fMRI analysis of the quiet mind. *Psychological Science* 21, no. 3 (2010): 322–328.

CHAPTER 1

1. Gollwitzer, Peter M., and Paschal Sheeran. Implementation intentions and goal achievement: A meta-analysis of effects and processes. *Advances in Experimental Social Psychology* (2006): 69–119. https://doi.org/10.1016/s0065-2601(06)38002-1.
2. Ellis, Rachel Reiff. Effects of parents' stress on a new baby. WebMD. (May 27, 2015). https://www.webmd.com/parenting/baby/features/stress-and-your-baby#1.
3. Coffey, John K. Cascades of infant happiness: Infant positive affect predicts childhood IQ and adult educational attainment. *Emotion* 20, no. 7 (2020): 1255–1265. https://doi.org/10.1037/emo0000640.
4. Brain Development. First Things First. (September 16, 2019). https://www.firstthingsfirst.org/early-childhood-matters/brain-development/.

CHAPTER 2

1. Hetland, Lois, and Kevin Wininger. The effects of loud music on auditory dependence. *Journal of Experimental Psychology: Human Perception and Performance* 27, no. 4 (2001): 817–826.
2. Dyall, Simon C. Long-chain omega-3 fatty acids and the brain: A review of the independent and shared effects of EPA, DPA and DHA. *Frontiers in Aging Neuroscience* 7 (2015). https://doi.org/10.3389/fnagi.2015.00052.
3. Asok, A., K. Bernard, T. L. Roth, J. B. Rosen, and M. Dozier. Parental responsiveness moderates the association between early-life stress and reduced telomere length. *Development and Psychopathology* 25, no. 3 (2013): 577–585. https://doi.org/10.1017/s0954579413000011.
4. Bernardi, L. Cardiovascular, cerebrovascular, and respiratory changes induced by different types of music in musicians and non-musicians: The importance of silence. *Heart* 92, no. 4 (2005): 445–452. https://doi.org/10.1136/hrt.2005.064600.
5. Buckner et al. The brain's default network: Anatomy, function, and relevance to disease. *Annals of the New York Academy of Sciences* 1124 (2008): 1–38.
6. Zeidan et al. Mindfulness meditation improves cognition: An fMRI analysis of the quiet mind. *Psychological Science* 24, no. 3 (2013): 322–328.
7. Luders et al. The effects of meditation on gray matter volume and cortical thickness: A systematic review, *NeuroImage* 82 (2013): 132–42.
8. Chopra, Deepak. *The Spontaneous Fulfillment of Desire*. New York: Harmony Books, 2005.
9. Watson, David, et al. The temperament and character inventory (TCI): Cross-cultural studies of personality traits and psychopathology. *Journal of Personality Disorders* 12, no. 4 (1998): 368–385.
10. Vandergrift, Larry, and Marzieh H. Tafaghodtari. Teaching L2 learners how to listen does make a difference: An empirical study. *Language Learning* 60, no. 2 (2010): 470–497. https://doi.org/10.1111/j.1467-9922.2009.00559.x.

CHAPTER 3

1. Collins, Nathan. How the human mind shapes reality. *Stanford News*, June 13, 2018. https://news.stanford.edu/2018/06/11/four-ways-human-mind-shapes-reality/.
2. Swart, Tara. *The Source: The Secrets of the Universe, the Science of the Brain*. HarperOne, 2019.

3. Neff, Kristin. Self-compassion. Self-compassion.org. https://self-compassion.org/ (accessed July 24, 2021).

CHAPTER 4

1. Norman-Haignere, S., N. G. Kanwisher, and J. H. McDermott. Distinct cortical pathways for music and speech revealed by hypothesis-free voxel decomposition. *Neuron, 88*(6) (2015): 1281–1296. https://doi.org/10.1016/j.neuron.2015.11.035.
2. Hallam, S., et al. The impact of music on psychological and cognitive processes: A systematic review. *Nature Reviews Neuroscience* 19, no. 3 (2018): 170–182.
3. Auto, Flávia Maria, Olga Maria Amancio, and Fernanda de Lanza. The effect of music on weight gain of preterm infants older than 32 weeks: A randomized clinical trial. *Revista Paulista de Pediatria* 33, no. 4 (2015). https://doi.org/10.1590/0103-058231369512.

CHAPTER 6

1. Ma, Xiao, Zi-Qi Yue, Zhu-Qing Gong, Hong Zhang, Nai-Yue Duan, Yu-Tong Shi, Gao-Xia Wei, and You-Fa Li. The effect of diaphragmatic breathing on attention, negative affect and stress in healthy adults. *Frontiers in Psychology* 8 (2017). https://doi.org/10.3389/fpsyg.2017.00874.
2. Sharma, Vivek Kumar, Madanmohan Trakroo, Velkumary Subramaniam, Ajit Sahai, Anand B. Bhavanani, and M. Rajajeyakumar. Effect of fast and slow pranayama on perceived stress and cardiovascular parameters in young healthcare students. *International Journal of Yoga* 6, no. 2 (2013): 104. https://doi.org/10.4103/0973-6131.113400.

CHAPTER 7

1. Kutchma, Teresa M. The effects of room color on stress perception: Red versus green environments. *Journal of Undergraduate Research* (Minnesota State University, Mankato): Vol. 3, Article 3 (2003).
2. Wolverton, B. C., Anne Johnson, and Keith Bounds. Interior landscape plants for indoor air pollution abatement. NASA (September 15, 1983).
3. Park, Bum Jin, Yuko Tsunetsugu, Tamami Kasetani, Takahide Kagawa, and Yoshifumi Miyazaki. The physiological effects of Shinrin-Yoku (taking in

the forest atmosphere or forest bathing): Evidence from field experiments in 24 forests across Japan. *Environmental Health and Preventive Medicine* 15, no. 1 (2009): 18–26. https://doi.org/10.1007/s12199-009-0086-9.

4. Strife, Susan, and Liam Downey. Childhood development and access to nature: A new direction for environmental inequality research. *Organization & Environment* 22, no. 1 (2009): 99–122. https://doi.org/10.1177/1086026609333340.

CHAPTER 8

1. Fomon, Samuel J. Infant feeding in the 20th century: Formula and Beikost. *The Journal of Nutrition* 131, no. 2 (February 2001):409S–420S. https://academic.oup.com/jn/article/131/2/409S/4686955#FN1.

2. Turner, Andrew. Concentrations and migratabilities of hazardous elements in second-hand children's plastic toys. *Environmental Science & Technology* 52, no. 5 (2018): 3110–3116. https://doi.org/10.1021/acs.est.7b04685.

3. Romeo, Rachel R., Julia A. Leonard, Sydney T. Robinson, Martin R. West, Allyson P. Mackey, Meredith L. Rowe, and John D. Gabrieli. Beyond the 30-million-word gap: Children's conversational exposure is associated with language-related brain function. *Psychological Science* 29, no. 5 (February 14, 2018): 700–710. https://doi.org/10.1177/0956797617742725.

4. Rochat, Philippe. Five levels of self-awareness as they unfold early in life. *Consciousness and Cognition* 12, no. 4 (2003): 717–731. https://doi.org/10.1016/s1053-8100(03)00081-3.

CHAPTER 9

1. Kuhl, P. K., F. M. Tsao, and H. M. Liu. Foreign-language experience in infancy: Effects of Chinese on phonological development. *Journal of the Acoustical Society of America*, 114, no. 5 (2003): 3026–3036.

2. Hirsh-Pasek, Kathy, Roberta Michnick Golinkoff, and Diane E. Eyer. A prescription for play. In *The Developing Brain*, edited by Marc H. Bornstein and Lea Davidson, 147–162 (New York: Guilford Press, 2015).

3. Zak, Paul. Why inspiring stories make us react: The neuroscience of narrative. *Cerebrum*, February 2015.

CHAPTER 10

1. Barbara H. Fiese and Thomas J. Tomcho. Finding meaning in family routines, *Journal of Family Psychology* 15, no. 4 (2001): 598–609.
2. Katz, L. F., J. M. Gottman, and C. Hooven. The meta-emotion interview: A clinical tool for assessing parental emotional awareness. In J. M. Gottman & J. J. Notarius (Eds.), *Clinical implications of research on parent-child interaction*, pp. 181–206 (New York: Guilford Press, 2012).
3. Huttenlocher, J. Synaptic density in human cerebral cortex. *Brain Research* 163, no. 2 (1979): 149–155.

CHAPTER 11

1. Norton, K. R., and G. M. Griffith. The impact of delivering mindfulness-based programmes in schools: A qualitative study. *Journal of Child and Family Studies* 29, no. 9 (2020): 2623–2636. https://doi.org/10.1007/s10826-020-01717-1.

CHAPTER 12

1. Dyer, N. L., A. L. Baldwin, and W. L. Rand. A large-scale effectiveness trial of reiki for physical and psychological health. *The Journal of Alternative and Complementary Medicine* 25, no. 12 (2019): 1156–1162. https://www.liebertpub.com/doi/full/10.1089/acm.2019.0022.

CHAPTER 13

1. Laakso, M., Åsa Fagerlund, S. Westerlund-Cook, et al. Enhancing mindfulness, emotional well-being, and strengths in parenting via an eight-week flourishing families intervention. *Journal of Child and Family Studies* 32, no. 8 (2023): 2375–2393. https://doi.org/10.1007/s10826-023-02618-9.

Index

baby-led weaning, 98, 118
bedtime, 161
breath, 10, 30, 65, 69–79, 85–86, 122, 124, 148–149, 156, 159, 183–184

circadian rhythm, 85, 116, 119, 138
cry, 19, 42, 66, 84, 103, 120, 131, 137, 140–141, 187
cues: emotional, 16; sleep, 141

diaper, x, 11, 19, 21, 33, 44–45, 49, 58, 65, 72, 82, 97, 106, 115, 118, 161, 181–183
direction, 32–33, 46

equanimity, 8, 18

feeding, 65, 72, 79, 90, 96, 98, 115, 117, 128–129, 133–134, 141, 157, 174, 177, 179, 180–181, 183, 189
Feng Shui, 82
focus: shifting 43

habit, 15, 17, 20, 23, 31, 88, 92, 98, 115, 120, 141–142, 168
healing touch, 144

intention, 31

kangaroo care. *See* skin-to-skin

manifesting, 63
meditation, 9
meltdown, 73, 155
monkey mind, 62
mood, 29, 42, 44, 52–54, 57, 60, 86, 101, 103–104, 140, 147

neuroplasticity, 29, 129

observation, 28

placebo effect, 40
plants, 86
playtime, x, 49, 73, 111, 161, 189

self-awareness, 100
self-care, 117
self-compassion, 48, 122, 169
sibling, 21, 162
skin-to-skin, 72, 132
sleep, 72; awake window, 141; cues, 141–142; ritual, 134; regression, 129

soothing, 132
stillness, 22
storytelling, 104, 133

trigger, 29

vibration, 53, 61, 64–65, 75, 78–79, 143–145, 148
visualization, 13

zen, xiii, 3, 166

About the Authors

Lindsay Ambrose is a trusted mindfulness educator and guide specializing in supporting families through transitions. As the founder of Positive Wellbeing LLC, she hosts the Life Recipes & Meditations Podcast and is the co-author of the books *Peaceful Mama* and *The Nurture Method*. Through her writing, speaking engagements, and one-on-one support, Lindsay empowers individuals, families, and communities to cultivate positive well-being through mindfulness, meditation, and spiritual growth. She holds an MA in writing and is certified as a postpartum doula and group facilitator. She serves as the administrator at Unity Spiritual Center in Oak Park while pursuing ministerial studies with a specialization in youth and family services. Learn more at LindsayAmbrose.com.

Arden Joy is an award-winning educator, author, and women's empowerment leader. She creates transformative resources that helps people to live authentically. As a certified yoga teacher and Reiki master, she weaves a unique holistic approach to cultivate mindfulness, celebrate diversity, and inspire a more wholehearted life. Arden's experiences as a queer, Jewish woman and mother of two—including a child with special needs—inform her work, infusing it with compassion, empathy, and inclusivity. Whether she is supporting her family in Chicago, her readers around the globe, or the 100,000 women in her Girls Who Travel online community, Arden invites others to join her on a journey of self-discovery and growth. You can learn more about Arden and her work at ArdenJoy.com.